///////////////////////////// Types of

Christian Theology /////////

///////////////////////////// Types of

Christian Theology //////////

Hans W. Frei

Edited by George Hunsinger
and William C. Placher

///////////// Yale University Press / New Haven and London

Published with assistance from the Louis Effingham deForest Memorial Fund.

Designed by Jill Breitbarth and set in Palatino type by Westchester Book/ Rainsford Type, Danbury, Connecticut.
Printed in the United States of America by BookCrafters, Inc., Chelsea, Michigan.

Library of Congress Cataloging-in-Publication Data
Frei, Hans W.
    Types of Christian theology / Hans W. Frei ; edited by George Hunsinger and William C. Placher.
        p. cm.
    Includes bibliographical references and index.
    ISBN 0-300-05104-2 (cloth)
            0-300-05945-0 (pbk.)
    1. Theology—Methodology—History. I. Hunsinger, George.
II. Placher, William C. (William Carl), 1948-   III. Title.
BR118.F75 1992
230'.01—dc20   91-34427
                                                                              CIP

The paper in this book meets the guidelines for permanence and durability of the Committee on Production Guidelines for Book Longevity of the Council on Library Resources.

10 9 8 7 6 5 4 3

Contents /////////////

Foreword ////////////

Hans W. Frei's projected history of Christology in the modern period was cut short by his death on 12 September 1988. It was to be a major project for which he had been preparing through most of his academic career, and those who knew him and his scholarship looked forward to it with high anticipation. As his friends and colleagues, we knew that he had worked out a typology by which to organize the material, and we knew that he had sketched some of what he wanted to say in the Shaffer Lectures he delivered at Yale Divinity School in 1983, in the Cadbury Lectures he delivered at the University of Birmingham in 1987, and in lectures he delivered in 1987 under the sponsorship of the Humanities Council at Princeton University. It was uncertain, however, in what condition the manuscripts were or whether any of them were publishable. His widow, Geraldine Frei, graciously consented to our sorting through her husband's papers to find these manuscripts. The three of us agreed to serve as a committee responsible for the final decision whether to seek to have them published. Professors George Hunsinger, Bangor Theological Seminary, and William Placher, Department of Religion, Wabash College, offered to collate and edit the papers, prepare them for publication, and introduce them. We are grateful for their painstaking care, patience, and excellent judgment. We are indebted to David Kamitsuka, who assisted Professor Frei, for help in identifying relevant papers. Although they are not the book Hans Frei set out to write, we believe these provocative essays are of considerable interest to students of modern Christian thought and ought to be publicly available.

DAVID KELSEY
GEORGE LINDBECK
GENE OUTKA

New Haven, Connecticut
January 1992

Editorial Introduction/////////////

When we undertook the task of assembling for publication Hans Frei's typology of modern Christian theology, we were acutely aware that the book Frei wished to write could no longer be written; we have thus decided to make available some obviously fragmentary manuscripts without disguising their unfinished character.

Frei's papers included a complete manuscript of the Shaffer Lectures as he had given them, nearly complete manuscripts of the Princeton lectures, parts of the Cadbury Lectures (some early fragments and then roughly the last three of his eight lectures), and a short grant proposal he had written to the National Endowment for the Humanities in the hope of funding a leave to work on the project. What happened to other manuscripts, particularly the rest of the Cadburys, remains a mystery. The lectureship manuscripts as we have them each develop the typology in part, yet none presents it as a whole. We have thus faced the task of reconstructing the overall plan by splicing together the materials at our disposal.

With funding from the Eric Dean Fund at Wabash College, a Wabash student, Jeffrey Marlett, typed the manuscripts (some in typescript, some handwritten) into a computer, so that we could begin editing them. It was, incidentally, somehow fitting that the work should be done at Wabash, where Frei had his first teaching job. We tried to keep our own editorial interference to a minimum. We cut some sections to avoid repetition and awkwardness, added some chapter and title headings, and, with the help of editors from Yale University Press, rewrote a few sentences for the sake of clarity. We also decided to keep editorial apparatus to a minimum. Frei sometimes gave full footnotes, sometimes a page number, sometimes no reference at all. We tried to complete the references and made other small alterations in the text without indicating them through the use of brackets. The manuscripts from which we worked will be available in the Yale library for scholars who want to check on details of the original text.

The grant proposal to NEH, an introduction to the whole project, constitutes chapter 1. Chapters 2 through 4 are the Shaffer lectures. Chapters 5 through 7 come from Cadbury material, edited to avoid repetition. They pick up where the Shaffer Lectures leave off, with further discussion of type 3 and then an account of types 4 and 5. Appendixes A and B are slightly edited versions of the Princeton lectures, which approach the same material from a different angle, with more emphasis on the historical and sociological context of the emergence of these types, a topic Frei was finding of growing importance in his thinking. Appendix C, Frei's review of Eberhard Busch's biography of Karl Barth, was originally published in the *Virginia Seminary Journal*, July 1978, pp. 42–46, and was reprinted in *Karl Barth in Review*, edited by H.-Martin Rumscheidt (Pittsburgh: Pickwick Press, 1981), pp. 95–116. It expands on the treatment of Barth in these manuscripts, and we thought republication here would make it more conveniently accessible.

Frei was a perfectionist, and in various ways these manuscripts do not meet his high standards for publication. The various parts were written for different occasions, and often in a rush. Frei was more informal in style, and sometimes more polemical, in oral presentation than he would have been in print. He may have changed his mind on some matters by the time of his death. His treatment of David Tracy here, for instance, rests primarily on *Blessed Rage for Order*. Tracy has shifted ground somewhat in later work, and Frei certainly grew very fond of him when Tracy taught for a semester at Yale. He might have been moved over to type 3.

Still, the manuscripts provide a major and original analysis of modern Christian theology. They have already been widely cited by people who have copies of the manuscripts or heard the lectures, and that is inevitably frustrating to those who do not have access to them. The issues of how and where one should do theology are widely debated these days, and the point of view Frei expresses here is too rarely heard. Frei always nervously rejected the idea of a "Yale school" of theology, but he influenced a great many students and colleagues, and reading his own work can make the nature of that influence clearer. For these reasons and others, publication seemed in order.

We are grateful to Geraldine Frei for giving permission for the project; to David Kelsey, George Lindbeck, and Gene Outka for their advice and support; to Jeff Marlett for all his work; to David Ford for lending his notes on the Cadbury Lectures, which enabled us to figure out which lectures our manuscripts represented, and for providing a transcript of a tape of a Cadbury fragment we did not have in manuscript; and to Bruce Marshall for identifying a long passage from his own work that Frei had quoted. We are, of course, above all grateful to Hans Frei, who influenced our work and our lives, as he did those of so many others.

GEORGE HUNSINGER
Bangor Theological Seminary

WILLIAM C. PLACHER
Wabash College

1 ///////////////////////////////// Proposal for a Project ////////////

I propose to complete a book on types of modern Christian thought, which will itself be part of a larger project on the figure of Jesus of Nazareth in England and Germany—in high culture, ecclesiastical and otherwise, as well as popular culture—since 1700.

Modern Western religious thought (and Christian thought as its chief instance) was shaped first in England and then in Germany, and the estimate of the person of Jesus has been at the heart of it. My present project is an attempt to sort out the varieties of high-culture religious rather than historical efforts during this period to arrive at such an estimate. Thus, I am writing a typology of modern Western Christian theology or theologies. This is a piece of conceptual analysis—that is, in principle an exercise chiefly *about* rather than *in* theology, although in practice the distinction will not always be clear. The ultimate aim of the work is to help provide conceptual orientation for a significant part of my larger historical project. In the meantime, I hope it will be a useful humanistic study in its own right—a richer guide to the varieties of thinking internal to this religion than some other typologies. First, such typologies have often been general without testing or focusing types on specific topics. Second, they have often been oversimplified and not sufficiently encompassing—for example, in calibrating a spectrum from radical to liberal to conservative or fundamentalist thought, or defining theological types by their outlook toward science, culture, or some other reified totality.

The status of Christianity in the modern West has been ambiguous: it has been viewed and has viewed itself both as an independent religious community or communities and as an official or at least privileged institution in the general cultural system, including the organization of learning and of thinking about the meaning of culture. This ambiguity is reflected in two very different, often contentious, but not

1

necessarily mutually exclusive views of Christian theology: (1) *Christian theology is an instance of a general class or generic type* and is therefore to be subsumed under general criteria of intelligibility, coherence, and truth that it must share with other academic disciplines. In the German term current since the end of the eighteenth century, its right to inclusion in a university curriculum depends on its exemplifying the criteria of validity set by a formal philosophical *Wissenschaftslehre*. (2) *Theology is an aspect of Christianity* and is therefore partly or wholly defined by its relation to the cultural or semiotic system that constitutes that religion. In this view theology is religion-specific, and whether or not other religions besides Christianity have theologies or something like them would have to be adduced case by specific case. In this view theology is explained by the character of Christianity rather than vice versa. Here Christian theology is first of all the first-order statements or proclamations made in the course of Christian practice and belief. But second—and more directly pertinent to this project—it is the Christian community's second-order appraisal of its own language and actions under a norm or norms internal to the community itself. This appraisal in turn has two aspects. The first is descriptive: an endeavor to articulate the "grammar," or "internal logic," of first-order Christian statements. The second is critical, an endeavor to judge any given articulation of Christian language for its success or failure in adhering to the acknowledged norm or norms governing Christian use of language.

In the first of these views of theology, the naturally cognate discipline to theology is philosophy—not only as transcendental analysis but as positive procedure in epistemology, ontology, and so on. In the second view, the natural external affiliate for second-order Christian communal self-description is not so much philosophy but interpretive (rather than reductionist or causally explanatory) social science, especially anthropology and sociology. What is at stake, externally or internally, is understanding a specific symbol system interpretively rather than reductively.

The typology I am proposing represents five different attitudes about these two descriptions of Christian theology, first of all in general and then in the way each type focuses on the topic of the *sensus literalis* with respect to the New Testament figure of Jesus.

In the first type, theology is a philosophical discipline within the academy, and its character as such takes complete priority over communal religious self-description within the religious group. The latter is, in fact, simply an instance of the former, and the distinction between external and internal description tends to disappear. Two examples would be Immanuel Kant and (in contemporary theology) Gordon Kaufman. In his proposals for the then projected new University of Berlin (1809), J. G. Fichte set forth this model as the only one under which a faculty of theology could be legitimately included in a modern university. The second type also claims the subsumption of theology under a general philosophical *Wissenschaftslehre*, but under the governing auspices of the latter it seeks to correlate specifically Christian with general cultural meaning structures such as natural science or the "spirit" of a cultural era. Among liberal theologians, Rudolf Bultmann, Wolfhart Pannenberg, and David Tracy exemplify this position, each in a very different way, and so does Karl Rahner in many of his philosophical-theological rather than his doctrinal writings; but, strikingly enough, so also do some conservative evangelical theologians like Carl Henry. External and internal descriptions of Christianity are two aspects whose conceptual convergence is made possible by the same underlying transcendental philosophical structure.

The third type also seeks to correlate theology as a procedure subject to formal, universal, and transcendental criteria for valid thinking, with theology as specific and second-order Christian self-description; but unlike the second type, it proposes no supertheory or comprehensive structure for integrating them, only ad hoc procedures: for example, broadly pragmatic appeals to the character of human experience. In my reading of them (which is controversial, since they can also be read under the second type), this is the outlook of Friedrich Schleiermacher and, to a lesser degree, Paul Tillich. Here the acquisition of *Christian knowledge* qua Christian self-description is as much a matter of learning a set of practical skills or capabilities as of learning a system of concepts under a general criterion of *meaning*. It was under this rather pragmatic rubric of correlating two different ways of learning without an integrating theory that Schleiermacher proposed that not only the faculty of theology but also those of two other practical arts directly useful to the public sector—law and medicine—be included in the plan of the University of Berlin, and his view rather than Fichte's prevailed.

The fourth type, like the third, argues that Christian theology is a nonsystematic combination of normed Christian self-description and method founded on general theory. But unlike the third, it does not propose a correlation between heterogeneous equals, and it reverses the priority ordering of the second type: the practical discipline of Christian self-description governs and limits the applicability of general criteria of meaning in theology, rather than vice versa. There can be no ultimate conflict between them, but in finite existence and thought we cannot know how they fit together in principle. As a result, Christian doctrinal statements are understood to have a status similar to that of grammatical rules implicit in discourse, and their relation to the broader or even universal linguistic or conceptual context within which they are generated remains only fragmentarily—perhaps at times negatively—specifiable; yet it is important to keep that relation open and constantly restate doctrinal statements in the light of cultural and conceptual change. The prime example of this type in twentieth-century theology is Karl Barth; in the nineteenth century John Henry Cardinal Newman bore at least a strong resemblance to it, as did Jonathan Edwards in the eighteenth.

For the fifth type, Christian theology is exclusively a matter of Christian self-description. External descriptive categories have no bearing on or relation to it at all. General theory is not pertinent to Christian self-description because there really is no such thing in any grand manner in the first place. "Languages" and their "grammars" always function in specific contexts. One learns the internal logic of any such context as one would a new language, through the acquisition of the appropriate conceptual skills, which are as much behavioral or dispositional as they are linguistic or descriptive. There is no formal, context-independent or independently describable set of transcendental conditions governing that internal logic. Christian theology is strictly the grammar of the faith, a procedure in self-description for which there is no external correlative. Examples of this outlook are a loosely knit group to whom the term "Wittgensteinian fideists" is sometimes applied; among them the religious philosopher D. Z. Phillips is perhaps the most prominent. But it is also a technical articulation of a religious outlook or sensibility that has a strong appeal to Christian evangelicals, for whom the language of the Bible is not so much factually correct as—much more importantly—inspired in its nurturing effect on the believer's heart. With its tendency to relegate doctrinal theology to a subordinate position, this outlook is a chameleon that can wear either conservative or liberal theological colors. Its technical articulation among theological or religious followers of Wittgenstein's later views is subject to some irony, for its sharp rejection of the other types is a purely philosophical rather than theological argument—namely, the rejection of universal, transcendental *Wissenschaftstheorie* and the appeal instead to the metaphor *grammar*. Opposite extremes sometimes tend to approach each other in circular fashion: the fifth type sometimes looks as philosophical as the first—not in what it affirms about Christianity but in what it appears to deny about the character of theology as part of Christianity.

How does each of these types bear on our central topic, on which there has in effect been something close to consensus in the major Christian theological traditions of the West—from their early history to their most recent liberal and conservative expressions? The central topic itself has two facets: (1) a consensus that in the interpretation of Scripture, especially the New Testament, the literal sense has priority over other legitimate readings, be they allegorical, moral, or critical; (2) a strong interconnection (which may even indicate derivation) between this priority of the literal sense and its application to the figure of Jesus Christ. "Literal sense" here applies primarily to the identification of Jesus as the *ascriptive* subject of the descriptions or stories told about and in relation to him—whether the status of this identification is that of chief character in a narrative plot, historically factual person, or reality under an ontological scheme. In other words, "literal" is not referentially univocal but embraces several possibilities. All other senses of the quite diverse and changing notion "literal" are secondary to this (to my mind, basic ascriptive Christological) sense of "literal," that the subject matter of these stories is not something or someone else, and that the rest of the canon must in some way or ways, looser or tighter, be related to this subject matter or at least not in contradiction to it. That is the minimal agreement of how "literal" reading has generally been understood in the Western Christian tradition. The consensus, then, covers the literal reading or meaning of the New Testament stories about Jesus in an ascriptive mode, but not the reality status of the ascriptive subject Jesus.

I shall try to demonstrate what I cannot expound at length here: that the third and fourth types are best designed to articulate the consensus in regard to this topical focus. Type 1 substitutes a general (religious, metaphysical, moral, existential, etc.) meaning for the specific ascriptive subject Jesus as the subject matter of the stories, a meaning of which the stories of Jesus are an example. Type 2 tries to have it both ways, especially in its liberal expressions: the meaning of the stories is at once a re-presentation of a (general or at least repeatable) experience or mode-of-being-in-the-world, but it is also the specific person Jesus of Nazareth. But this endeavor at "second naïveté" or a revised literal reading (David Tracy, under the hermeneutical tutelage of Paul Ricoeur) either reverts to the views on the matter of the first type or else simply ends in hermeneutical incoherence. Type 3 customarily articulates the literal ascriptive sense by correlating a description of the "Jesus of history" with one of the "Jesus Christ of faith," remaining hermeneutically consistent but risking contradiction in the endeavor of integrating theological description with historical method. Type 4 successfully asserts the unity of the ascriptive Christological subject at the hermeneutical level but cannot specify the mode or manner in which Christological statements are "historical," while nonetheless asserting that they are. Type 5 is reduced to hermeneutical silence—that is, simply repeating the scriptural statements and then, instead of interpreting them under a literal (or some other) reading, claiming that "understanding" these statements is simply equivalent to acquiring the (religious) skill or capacity to use them in the appropriate manner.

The third and fourth types—represented by Schleiermacher and Barth—usually thought to be at opposite poles, are very close under this typology and its chief topical center. Between them they best exhibit both the possibilities and the problems of significant second-order restatement of the tradition of the major hermeneutical and theological consensus in Western Christianity. While each of the types will obviously have its place in the larger historical project, these two will raise the most intense issues in the developing high-culture Christian thought of the modern period. It is easy enough to fix, for example, Deist and Pietist responses to the consensus about the figure of Jesus; it is more challenging to ferret out what those in between were saying.

The historical, hermeneutical, and theological views developed in this study are a continuation as well as revision of two previous efforts, *The Identity of Jesus Christ* (a hermeneutical and exegetical study)[1] and *The Eclipse of Biblical Narrative* (a conceptual-historical study in hermeneutics up to 1835).[2] In two recent essays I have further focused this work: one is historical and implies that for the history of Christian thought the conceptual issue in Christology, that is, the nature of the unitary ascriptive subject, ought to have priority over the historical

one, that is, the relation of historical and theological methods. David
Friedrich Strauss was important because in effect he reversed this
logical sequence.[3] In a theological essay I argue that the *sensus literalis*
is incompatible with the phenomenological hermeneutics of Paul Ricoeur and David Tracy (type 2, above) if that position is regarded as
having "foundational status."[4]

I hope this book will be important not only in that it provides conceptual structure within a historial project, but also simply in its own
right as a proposal to view Christianity as one religion among others—
that is, as a semiotically coherent cultural system. In this way the cause
of comparative religions can be served better than by interpreting
Christianity (or any other religion) *exclusively* from within the matrix
of its (secular or sacral) cultural setting.

The general theme of these chapters is Jesus Christ and interpretation. The book will be a reflection in theology, and more or less a reflection in modern theology; for being an academician by nature and vocation, I find that certain themes in modern academic theology have set me to thinking. One of them is a kind of informal agreement at least among Protestants, and probably among Roman Catholic theologians also, that the central persuasion of Christian theology, not so much to be defended as to be set out, is that Jesus Christ is the presence of God in the Church to the world.

In the eighteenth century the doctrine of Jesus Christ was conceived as a doctrine of revelation, the communication of doctrinal truth, to the effect that Jesus was the unique revealer or revelation of God. In the nineteenth century the theological procedure changed, and there was more and more of a reflection by theologians on religion and its character as a permanent, native human state. But when it came to the *Christian* religion there was a kind of consensus that it had one doctrine to which all the others were related, like spokes to the center of a wheel. Whatever one's theological method, however one proceeded to think about theology, the content seemed to be reflection on Jesus Christ as Incarnate Lord and as Redeemer of the human race. For a while it seemed that somebody in the nineteenth century had demonstrated the necessity and rationality of the idea of Incarnation and Reconciliation—his name was Hegel, and he has been a plague ever since—but nobody took it altogether literally. But in the theological and professional guild, reflection on Jesus Christ took another turn, a turn that was verbally, and probably substantively too, announced by David Friedrich Strauss. He asked, What is the relation of the Jesus of history—that is, the Jesus given to us in the texts and truly rendered for us, he thought, by the historian's accurate, factual reconstruction of what is reported in those texts—to the Christ of faith, the Christ who is believed to be Redeemer in the Church?

Now three subquestions in that respect. Was the Jesus portrayed in the Gospels the real historical Jesus? In other words, were the reports accurate? Second, was the Christ in that portrayal the one of whom it should be said, "Art thou he who is to come, or are we to wait for another?" In other words, ought one to think that he thought of himself as the Christ? Third, if the answer is yes, he thought of himself that way, is the portrayal a piece of mythologizing about a charismatic figure or is it to be taken literally? If, as a Christian and a theologian, you answer yes to the second and third of these three questions about the relation of the historical Jesus to the Christ of faith—that is, if you say he is the one that was to come, we do not have to wait for another—then you ask where is the unity to be found between the Jesus of history and Christ of faith, both in the New Testament accounts and in principle.

These questions then lead to others. First of all, where in the *portrait* is the unity? Is it, as some historians and many theologians thought—that's the way they thought historical investigation and theological persuasion came together—in his messianic self-consciousness? But then the question arose, do we have access to his inner being from the text? There was a famous argument at the end of the nineteenth century between those (for example, Wilhelm Wrede and a little later Rudolf Bultmann) who said that the messianic secret in Mark was not that of Jesus at all, but that of the gospel writer, and others (for example, Albert Schweitzer and Johannes Weiss) who said no, Jesus himself held the messianic secret. Later there were those who asked, Is the messianic secret, the conjunction of true historical reports and the true being of Jesus, in his *words* perhaps rather than in his self-consciousness? Is that the locus of the unity we can arrive at by historical investigation as well as by religious persuasion? Is it in the words that that unity lies? Jesus is a *Word Event*, or his own performative utterance. But then the question is, of course, what words can we take to be absolutely reliable if we are historians?

And then there were those who said, well, whether he himself or his followers thought of him as the Messiah, messianic claims were a dime a dozen in that area at that time. There are parallels all about. Among those who said that there was something distinctive about Jesus, there were those who claimed that you could find it by looking at the texts as sources, and there were those who said no, historical work did not get you either to the Jesus in back of the texts, or to what is unique about him, because by definition historical method cannot render someone who is an exception to the rules under which the method works. If you are going to investigate Jesus historically, the "real" historical Jesus, then by definition he won't be unique, he cannot be the Christ. It is forbidden not only by the outcome of the actual historical investigation but also by the assumptions of historical method, which arranges events into a naturally explicable sequence of similar occurrences. But then there were those who said that just for that reason, we ought to separate historical investigation entirely from the inquiry into faith that constitutes theology. The best we can do for theology by way of historical inquiry is to show that historical investigation of the Gospels eventuates in skepticism about our knowledge of the figure of Jesus: we can get back by way of the writings of the New Testament to the faith of the early Christian community in him, but not to himself. At the same time we can say that there is a unique access to Jesus as Redeemer—a unique method if you will: faith is a unique road to the apprehension of Christ. This combination was the path of the dialectical theology, the early Barth and the constant Bultmann. And people on the other side said, you cannot both claim that a figure is historical *and* that in principle you cannot have a historian's access to him. The people who said that were David Friedrich Strauss, Ernst Troeltsch, and Van Harvey in our day.

Historians seem to tell us that the only way you can get to Jesus and have whatever religion you may after that is by having religion transmitted to us by experts, by way of historical results, which is surely not very satisfactory to any of us. I think most of us have some hunch that we can actually read the Bible, including the New Testament, and that it isn't absolutely essential to have the experts tell us what we can find there. Opposing Strauss and his descendants, the dialectical theologians who made an absolute split between faith and history and were energetically pursuing the special way of access by way of faith invoked the ghost of Søren Kierkegaard and the claim to the disciple's contemporaneity with Christ. Kierkegaard had been ignored in his own day, and he was now posthumously elected professor in any given theological faculty, at which appointment I suspect, just as much as at the use these people made of him, the flesh-and-blood figure of Søren Kierkegaard would have smiled.

But I want to return to another ghost, one I mentioned earlier: that of David Friedrich Strauss. Strauss was one of those who believed that one's religious belief in Christ ought to await the historical experts' verdict. He said, "The critical examination of the life of Jesus is the test of the dogma of Christ." Then he went on to say that the dogma fails the test. Later in life, he said, "The illusion, which is supported primarily by Schleiermacher's explanations, that Jesus could have been a man in the full sense and still as a single person stand above the whole of humanity, is the chain which still blocks the harbor of Christian theology against the open sea of rational science."[1] Karl Barth comments that, together with Ludwig Feuerbach, David Friedrich Strauss, in the passage just quoted, constitutes the bad conscience of modern theology, and that the historical question was put by Strauss with unparalleled force. After Barth had written these words and added, "In order to understand Strauss's historical question, you must love that question,"[2] he went on to say that true theology begins precisely where the problems discovered by Feuerbach and Strauss are seen—the skeptical historical problem that you cannot get the Christ of faith out of the supposed Jesus of history—and then laughed at. Van Harvey, a modern Strauss, quotes that remark and asks if that laughter is not perhaps gallows humor.

The whole of which these chapters are part is a plodding inquiry into what it might mean to laugh, but to laugh fairly and not sarcastically, and not in a fashion that might turn to gallows humor. Thus, I will for the most part be asking, Just what is Christian theology? How is it related to other things, like, say, historical science? and How does theological reflection bear on the reading of the New Testament texts about Jesus Christ? though notice I am not saying that I will give an exegesis.

The whole project looks something like this. I am persuaded that historical inquiry is a useful and necessary procedure but that theological reading is the reading of the *text*, and not the reading of a *source*, which is how historians read it. Historical inquiry, while telling us many useful things, does not tell us how we are to understand the texts as texts. I am persuaded that in the search for an answer to the question of how to understand the texts as texts, the closest discipline to theology is not history at all. When I ask what external discipline is potentially most useful to theology, I come up with an answer that surprises me, and it is a certain kind of social anthropology that bears some relationship to a kind of literary inquiry also. Why? Because I take it that Christianity, on which theology reflects, is first of all a religion. It is not a network of beliefs, it is not a system, first of all. It may be an intellectual system also, but not in the first place. Further, it is not first of all an experienced something, an experienced shape, an essence. Rather, it is first of all a complex, various, loosely held, and yet really discernible community with varying features—a religious community of which, for example, a sacred text is one feature; that is typical of a religion. And the sacred text usually (and certainly in Christianity), in the tradition of interpretation within the religion, comes to focus around a sacred story. The word *sacred* is terribly loaded; let's simply say it focuses around a *central* story, certainly in the Christian religion, in the Christian community. It is this kind of approach that I discern in looking at religion, the Christian religion, not under any high-powered comparative system, but under the aegis of that rather humdrum science, anthropology.

The kind of anthropology I'm thinking of may be distinguished by two highly illuminating terms that Professor Paul Ricoeur has used: it has a hermeneutics—that is, a theory of interpretation—not of *suspicion* but of *restoration*. A hermeneutics of suspicion is a theory of interpretation that says that every self-interpretation of a religion and other social phenomena is really an ideology—that is to say, the self-interpreters don't really know what it's about. It's only the intelligent outside observer who knows what the real thing is because he has an explanatory structure for it. The self-interpreters fool themselves; so, for example, for Emile Durkheim, the real object of totem-worshiping people (which the primitives themselves can't know) is society, which only a modern scientific observer of their religion can find out. Sigmund Freud, Karl Marx, and Emile Durkheim are the principal "hermeneuticians of suspicion" with regard to religion in general and Christianity in particular.

There is another and different kind of interpretation that is rather closer to self-interpretation, a hermeneutics of restoration, an interpretation that does not operate with an explanatory hypothesis to nearly the same sweeping degree as the hermeneutics of suspicion does. The kind of social anthropology I'm thinking of is exemplified by Clifford Geertz's essay, "Thick Description: Towards a Theory of Interpretation of Cultures,"[3] which is close to self-interpretation, though from the outside. Rather than *explaining* the culture that one looks at, one tries to *describe* it. Culture is a kind of natural convention, and studying it is called ethnography. It's a way really of finding our footing with a group of strangers who have a common sign system, verbal but perhaps also ritual—a semiotic system within which we try then to orient ourselves. Geertz uses an example that he borrowed from Gilbert Ryle, that you cross from nature into culture when you understand the difference, which you can't understand at a physiological level, between a wink and a blink. A blink is physiologically exactly the same thing as a wink, but a wink, unlike a blink, is something you do under rules. It's a communication, a small communications system. You know what you're doing when you're winking, and so does the other person. It's part of an intricate and elaborate game with rules to it. Geertz suggests that you can see this system from the agent's or player's point of view, so that there's a difference but also a subtle connection, a transition, between outsider and insider. You see it from the agent's point of view without becoming a native or without mimicking him. There used to be a description of the extended New Guinea aboriginal family: it consists of father, mother, children, aunts, cousins, and the Harvard anthropologist who is living with them, doing his fieldwork. That's precisely what you do *not* have here. You do not mimic and you do not become a native.

> Culture consists of socially established structures of meaning, in terms of which people do such things as signal conspiracies and join them, or perceive insults and answer them.[4]

> As interworked systems of construable signs . . . culture is not a power, something to which social events, behaviors, institutions or processes can be causally attributed; it is a context, something within which they can be intelligibly—that is, thickly—described.[5]

It is very reminiscent of what Wittgenstein called a language game.

I'm suggesting very simply that the Church is like that—a culture, not only of course for the observer but also for the agent, the adherent, who would understand it. There is a sacred text—a typical element in a religious system—and there are informal rules and conventions governing how the sign system works in regard to sacred scripture. The kind of theology that I like best is the kind that is closer to this outlook rather than to philosophy, or to historiography, although it is impossible to avoid philosophy. You may not even want to, but that's a story for another time.

The rules—the formal or, more likely, informal rules that the members of the community follow with regard to the reading of the sacred text—are most likely to have been learned in or by application. They have to be applied in terribly different situations, so they can't be rigid, especially because they have to cover two different, on the face of it, sets of writings: an earlier Jewish scripture which, in the process of being united with the later set we distort from Jewish scripture into something that is called the Old Testament (if it is a distortion!). But in view of the different situations in which the rules have to be applied, and in view of the two sets of writings, the rules have to be flexible. In the process of developing these rules in the West, in Western Christianity in particular, one guideline came to be basic: Whenever possible use the literal sense, although the allegorical or spiritual sense is permissible where the literal leaves you in the dark, or where the text says something that, when taken literally, is unworthy of God.

But the literal sense is not a single thing. (For a beautiful article that explains something of the history of that sense, see Brevard Childs's "The Sensus Literalis of Scripture: An Ancient and Modern Problem.")[6] It is, however, astonishing how much continuity there is, even though the literal sense is not the same throughout the history of the interpretive tradition. For example, with regard to the modern technical discussion of the relationship between the Jesus of history and the Christ of faith, it turns out that much of it is a modern continuation of the older tradition of the literal sense, even for the most liberal scholars. For in modernity, beginning in about the eighteenth century, among Christian scholars and scholars loosely attached to the Christian tradition, the literal sense came to mean that sense which you had when you took the texts to give you an accurate picture of what actually transpired—that is, when you knew not simply what the text was saying, and took that literally rather than allegorically, but rather when you transposed that literal sense into a literal or accurate description of that to which it referred: the "events," the "facts." Modern theology took its cue from much of modern science and philosophy, and so became obsessed with the notion and discernment of true factuality. "Facticity," or "factuality," came to be a kind of a magic word, and theoreticians would clobber each other with it. In a situation where facts are facts and you have ways of investigating and ascertaining them, the *sensus literalis*, the literal sense, comes to be that meaning of the text, that verbal description which is in accurate accord with the facts. And make no mistake about it, liberals were as concerned about this—and they worked from that same kind of thought structure—as fundamentalists, except that liberals located, in the case of the Gospels, the ascribed person differently than fundamentalists did. By and large, liberals said that Jesus Christ had a time-conditioned self-consciousness, which fundamentalists of course would not admit. Working with a time-conditioned self-consciousness, you are at liberty to see much of what he says in those terms, but there comes a point when the jig is up, when you can't pass the buck. For liberals too, at some point, there has to be a coincidence of accuracy between the text and something with regard to the historical Jesus to which the text refers.

Since I have used the term *literal sense*, let me quickly say a few things about it. It changes so much—actually it doesn't mean one thing—that I'm not at all sure that I want to try and give a specific definition. It can't be done. But here are some rough rules, and one of them may be a little surprising. The first one that I want to draw attention to is one that has been noted by a distinguished Jewish scholar, Raphael Loewe, in talking about Jewish scripture, and more recently by Charles Wood in *The Formation of Christian Understanding;*[7] it states that the literal meaning of the text is precisely that meaning which finds the greatest degree of agreement in the use of the text in the religious community. If there is agreement in that use, then take that to be the literal sense. The point here is that the greatest degree of agreement on the applicability of the literal sense, whatever it might be, was in regard to the person of Jesus in the texts. No wonder, then, that if this was the focus of agreement, it became a kind of center for the literal sense from which literal reading radiated outward to other parts of the New Testament. So the first sense of the literal reading stems from the use of the text in the Church.

The second rule concerning the literal sense is that it is the fit enactment of the intention to say what comes to be in the text. This understanding of the literal sense does not say that the text wrote itself, and that therefore you can take it simply as it is—no, there's an admission by and large that texts are written by authors, human, or divine, for that matter. But what is interesting is that the intention and its enactment are thought of as one continuous process—one intelligent activity, not two—so that you cannot for this purpose go behind the written text to ask separately about what the author meant or what he or she was really trying to say. You had better take it that the author said what he or she was trying to say.

The third rule has to do with the descriptive fit between the words and the subject matter, and thereby hangs a very long story—alas, it's a deep problem that I won't even try to avoid, although I shall postpone dealing with it as long as I can. How we know about that "fit" is one of the questions raised by the study called hermeneutics. (Hermeneutics means simply "theory of interpretation," though it has been expanded to mean all sorts of other things. Hermeneutics, by and large, is a word that is forever chasing a meaning. But one of the things that it investigates is, How do we know when we have a coincidence between the semantic whole—the sentence, the paragraph, the semantic continuum—and the subject matter? How do we know when we have a fit, correspondence, or coincidence between sense and meaning? Or, to quote Professor Ricoeur again, How do we know when we have a harmony between the *what* of the text and the *about what* of the text?) The literal sense, in my mind, is one that asserts not only the co-incidence between sense and subject matter, but may even, as a matter of hermeneutical principle, go further and suggest that we may be asking a misplaced question when we make a sharp distinction between sense and subject matter. I will return to this issue later. But the two latter points, intention-enactment and the harmony between sense and subject matter, have been the subject of interpretive theory. They have been dealt with especially in a tradition that has deep ties with nineteenth-century philosophy and theology, a tradition of which I take Paul Ricoeur to be the finest representative. By and large, in this tradition meaning and understanding are two permanently fixed, mutually involved terms that describe a kind of dialectical process into which all actual work of interpretation somehow has to fit. "Meaning" is an objective universal, and "understanding," its transcendental condition of possibility.

Other hermeneuticians have suggested that understanding is not one thing but many, depending on what you are working at, and that you should not ask at all what it means to understand a text—or, correspondingly, what is the meaning of a text—but rather how is the text used and in what context. That is a better, less abstract question than What is the meaning of the text? and What does it mean to understand a text? as though that were always one and the same thing. Yet it is possible that, although one prefers to look at use, there is a residual "meaning" game.

Then there are those in our own day who suggest that both ways of looking at the principles of interpretation are utterly wrong-headed. These people say we ought not even raise the question of "use," and that to use the very term *meaning* is already to be engaged in a kind of unintelligible global speculation. In saying this, they suggest a very curious thing: namely, that the way to understand a text is not by principles of interpretation but by a kind of thick tradition of reading, very much like that of Midrash; that it is not that the text fits into a contextual, nontextual world in which it "means" or does not "mean," or that it is a text that can be used within such a world, but rather that the world, any "world," should be understood on the model of "text," and that reading therefore constitutes a more profound and genuine use of language than speaking in dialogue or communicating in a common world. The best-known proponent of this view is Jacques Derrida.

Why stress these things? Because it is in these terms that the discussion over the literal sense has recently taken place, and it is in these terms that that discussion is at present undergoing a strange turn. We learned in theology to try to come to terms positively or negatively with what historians were doing. Then there seemed to be a moment of liberation from being completely restricted to historical questions and to the supposed bedrock issues of "faith" and "history", when people arose who said that the Bible should be read as a piece of literature—as text, not as source—and that literary reading therefore gets us closer to what theologians ought to be saying than the historians do. But now, the literary readers of the text have mounted a deliberate assault on the literal sense, which they take to be the predominant mode of interpretation in the Church. Some of the literary readers are saying (I'm thinking particularly of Frank Kermode, *The Genesis of Secrecy*)[8] that when the Christians adopted Jewish scripture and turned it into an Old Testament, they did so by force. In point of fact, that is how we always deal with earlier texts. We read them by force (a point on which Kermode agrees with Harold Bloom), and, he says, it is high time to use the force which the Christians used on Jewish scripture and turn it on the Christian scripture. If one does that, he says in a kind of afterword, the enemy to be smitten is the literal sense. It is precisely for this reason that he chooses for his assault Mark's parable of the sower, in which Jesus tells his disciples that he speaks to the outsiders in parables in order that seeing they may not see, and hearing they may not understand. A parable does not open up; a parable closes. A parable is a puzzle; it is precisely that which *prevents* literal reading. And for that reason, among others, both internal reasons of the Church and external reasons of conversation with others, the literal sense becomes an overwhelmingly important issue.

Let me take you now on what I fear is a dreary little trip through modern theology. The landscape is not particularly fascinating, but it must be traversed. Keeping in mind this question, "What kind of theology is most nearly hospitable to the literal sense of Scripture?" let us proceed.

3 ///////////////////// Theology, Philosophy, and Christian Self-Description /////////////,

I propose to draw a brief map of modern theology, chiefly Protestant, largely for purposes of locating the spot from which I believe one can most productively explore the relation of hermeneutics—that is, theory of interpretation—not so much to biblical interpretation itself as to the Christian religion. The map I shall draw is not impartial; it is more like the *New Yorker's* notorious map of the United States—in which New York City eclipses the Midwest and allows only a glimpse of the West Coast, with China just beyond—than like a segment from the U.S. Geological Survey. Such maps are called typologies; they're nothing to be particularly proud of, but they do have a limited use in projecting innocent people into the author's secret mountain retreat or underground cave, so that if they want to get out and go on from there, they'll have to use their own compass and their own ingenuity. The irony of such a mapping enterprise is that it is concerned with something called "theological method"—in other words, not so much with doing theology as asking what it is and how one would go about it if one were to do it. Somebody rightly said, "A person either has character or he invents a method." I believe that and have been trying for years to trade method for character, since at heart I really don't believe in independent methodological study of theology (I think the theory is dependent on the practice), but so far I haven't found that I'm a seller to myself as a purchaser.

For centuries, institutions of higher learning in Western culture were governed by the organization of learning into the study of the liberal arts, the *trivium* and *quadrivium*, and theology on top of them. Theology in that context is discourse about a concept, "God," and the usual assumption has been that part of what the inquiry is about is whether or not or how the concept "refers." On the one hand, theology has been a generally accessible subject matter, broadly based, both as a

19

technical concept and as a wider cultural one: "God" and perhaps God, even if there may be arguments about distinctive conditions required to enable one to get into a position to study it, him, or her. On this view, theology and philosophy are bound to be closely if perhaps oddly related. Philosophy may be an informative science, which tells you, for example, what being is, and how you get into a position to know it, and in what respects God has or is being, and in what respects he or she surpasses it. But in addition—or, perhaps, alternatively—philosophy may be regarded as being a foundational discipline which, rather than giving us information, provides us with the criteria of meaning and certainty, coherence as well as truth, in any arena of human reflection. In other words, the rules of correct thought are invariant and all-fields-encompassing. In the light of its foundational status, philosophy arbitrates what may at any time and anywhere count as meaningful language, genuine thought, and real knowledge. And theology, given its long but also dubious standing in the academy, is a prime candidate for philosophical scrutiny.

On the other hand, Christianity is a specific religion among many others, a religious community called after its founder, whose name, Jesus of Nazareth, is linked to the title embodying the claim his followers made on his behalf, that he was the Christ. In this context, theology is a very different matter. In the previous case, the phrase *Christian theology* was used to give an instance of a general kind of undertaking—namely, a Christian instance. But now theology becomes an aspect of the self-description of Christianity as a religion, rather than an instance in a general class. It is an inquiry into the internal logic of the Christian community's language—the rules, largely implicit rather than explicit, that are exhibited in its use in worship and Christian life, as well as in the confessions of Christian belief. Theology, in other words, is the grammar of the religion, understood as a faith and as an ordered community life.

Whether and to what extent other religions also have theologies in this sense of the word is, as I said earlier, a matter for case-by-case comparison. One of the characteristics of Christian theology is that one can discover at least three aspects to it, all of which tend to blend into each other. First, there is what we might call first-order theology— that is, Christian witness, including the confession of specific beliefs (for example, the creeds) that seem on the face of them to be talking about acknowledging a state of affairs that holds true whether one believes it or not. But second, there is what we have just called the logic, or grammar, of the faith, which may well have bearing on the first-order statements, an endeavor to bring out the rules implicit in first-order statements. And third, there is a kind of quasi-philosophical or philosophical activity involved even in this kind of theologizing, which consists of trying to tell others, perhaps outsiders, how these rules compare and contrast with their kinds of ruled discourse. But certainly in first- and second-order talk, perhaps even in third-, detaching the rules governing the use of the language of the religion from its illustration is the wrong way to go about things. But the really important thing is to know that even such distinctions are not *prescriptive*, that their sometimes quite natural violation in practice says nearly as much about them as the distinctions say themselves.

Schleiermacher speaks of Christian theology as being of this second sort when he calls it the comprehensive concept of all those scientific skills and rules without whose use a coherent governance of the Christian Church—that is, an ecclesiastical regimen—is impossible. He assigns it the role of a "positive" science, and the distinction is clearly the one I have just made.

When we say that Christian theology in this mode is critical or normed Christian self-description, we are obviously putting it in a very different context from the previous, philosophical one. The ambiguity may be a blessing, a curse, or a bit of both. In any event, it is probably built into the religion itself, with its well-known problematic penchant for making universal truth claims, establishing normative guidelines for interpretation, and so on, while it is at the same time a particular social phenomenon rather than a metaphysical construct or an ontological vision.

But now a further question: Is theology, as reflection on the ruled use of the Christian community's language, completely internal to that community? Or is self-description here either comparable to another kind of description, though not identical with it, or is it part of some other description? The answer of course depends on whom you are asking. There are those who say, yes, it is completely internal and there is no use in comparing Christian discourse and its rules with other kinds of discourse. Then there are those who propose that while locating Christian language certainly is not a direct philosophical task, since Christianity is a religion, it may be described under the same rubrics in which other religions are described. And here one faces two options. First, there are some who believe that religion is a component of human experience and that this experience is a primordial element in the human constitution. It is not something that can be ferreted out by ordinary examination for information, but rather it is part of the structure of the human psyche with which we come to grips when we come to grips with the things that are actually given to the human psyche. The other option is that a religion is best described by the social sciences, and that therefore theology as the grammar of the faith is closer to the social sciences than to philosophy, though certainly not identical with them. Christianity is a religion, a social organism. Its self-description marks it typically as a religion in a way similar to those descriptions given by sociologists of religion or cultural anthropologists. It is a community held together by constantly changing, yet enduring structures, practices, and institutions, as other religious communities are: for example, a sacred text, regulated relations between an elite (overlapping but not identical with a professional group) and more general body of adherents, a set of rituals—preaching, baptism, the celebration of communion, common beliefs and attitudes—all of which are linked (again typical of a religion) with a set of narratives connected with each other in the sacred text and its interpretive tradition. All of these components are, for social scientist and theologian, not the *signs* or *manifestations* of the religion; they constitute it in complex and changing coherence.

The previous kind of description of religion as experience (let us call it phenomenological) sees a whole-making capacity in the structure of the psyche that does the experiencing. The religion is constituted by an experienced unity, or essence, of which all these external, social aspects are signs and manifestations rather than being the religion as such. One may suspect that the phenomenological description of specific religions comes closer to the philosophical kind of theologizing than does a social science kind of description. So while one may want to distance oneself from both of them, as not being substitutes for Christian self-description, the social scientific description of Christianity may come closer to a self-description of Christianity than does the phenomenological one. It may or it may not. For on the other hand, perhaps "inside" description can only be rendered if one agrees that there is an "inside" to a religion, and the experience-reporters claim that they do justice to that fact, and perhaps they best of all. It all depends on whom you ask, both inside and outside the theological guild. But there is another candidate for the specific description of Christianity, a candidate whom theologians in the nineteenth century, but also in this one, have used frequently, in order both to give a description of Christianity as a specific religion, and to constitute a bridge, if not do service for, Christian self-description. And that is history. Intellectual historians or historians of dogma have found it tempting to say that the history of Christianity, especially the history of its articulated beliefs or doctrines, presents amidst all its changes a cumulative story in which a certain central essence (once again!) or continuity of ideas and outlooks can be distinguished from what is merely temporary or peripheral. The history of dogma, far from being what D. F. Strauss called it, the dissolution of dogma, is in reality the story of the clarification of the central and abidingly meaningful character of Christianity. The historian of dogma had a next-door neighbor, the historian of religions, who did not agree but insisted on throwing bricks through his neighbor's windows. He thought that there was no distinctive essence of anything over a period of historical development, that essence in history is change. You showed that every seemingly distinctive characteristic of a religion had nearby or faraway parallels, and when all the parallels were thrown into the melting pot of time, nobody had anything distinctive left anyway.

How have Christian theologians, mainly those of the Protestant variety, looked at relations or lack of relations between the two ways of thinking about theology? I want to try to exemplify five types of views on this matter. It will not be done very cleanly because all sorts of other considerations will intrude. One ought to be mentioned because it will constantly upset the smooth surface of an ideal typology with the ugly interruptions of real theologizing, and that is a pity. First of all, the writings of Protestant theologians throughout eighteenth-, nineteenth-, and twentieth-century theology have come to constitute a kind of canon. And for the most part the texts in that canon have two characteristics in common. First, it turns out to be the fact that even though most of their writers were genuinely concerned about the Church, they were academic theologians, and they never forgot it. Even when they spoke as Christian self-describers, they did it in a very academic way. But even more important is the fact that they tended to give the edge to the philosophical kind of theology—that is, to the kind of theology that was related to philosophy as the nearest fellow discipline in the academy. They did it most often by couching even specific descriptions of Christianity in formal and universal gauges or measures or criteria of what constitutes intelligible procedure—that is, in philosophical criteria. So the typology cuts right across the ordinary lines of liberal and conservative. For example, a contemporary liberal theologian like David Tracy of the University of Chicago will look more like a conservative and evangelical theologian such as Carl Henry than he will like many a fellow liberal in regard to the basic affirmation that theology must have a foundation that is articulated in terms of basic philosophical principles. The terminology may be different, but they say much the same thing in some respects. Thus Henry says, "Since revelation is itself conceptual and verbal, no arbitrary boundary can be erected between philosophy and theology, and philosophy can enrich itself from the content of revealed theology. For theology and philosophy are active on the same terrain."[1] Furthermore, Henry criticizes Karl Barth severely for refusing to submit theology to common logical criteria, such as the law of contradiction, the so-called congruity postulate, and the criterion that all propositions must be arrangeable in the form of axioms and theorems, the criterion that coherence obeys the same rules everywhere, and so on, and so on.[2] In a very similar vein, though with very different concrete philosophical filling, David Tracy calls reflective discipline capable of such inquiry " 'transcendental' in its modern formulation or 'metaphysical' in its more traditional expression. . . . such reflection attempts the explicit mediation of the basic presuppositions . . . that are the conditions of the possibility of our existing or understanding at all. . . . The task of fundamental theology can only be successfully resolved when the theologian . . . develops an explicitly metaphysical study of the cognitive claims of religion and theism as an integral moment in his larger task."[3] And in line with this ambitious agenda (what are the basic conditions of all human living and thinking? is what he wants to square theology with) he adduces a set of a priori criteria of accuracy and appropriateness, of meaning, meaningfulness, and truth—all of them explicitly philosophical and independent of application, all similar to Henry's agenda. The similarity extends to the informational side of philosophy also, though Henry is directly metaphysical, whereas Tracy is so indirectly, by way of speculative metaphysics.

If the concern for philosophy as foundational to theology is one confusing factor for the usual liberal-conservative distinction, the other characteristic of the canon of modern theology supplements it obliquely in a way that also influences our typology. This one has less to do with philosophy and more with an abiding puzzle within the history of theology. Ever since the later Middle Ages, it has been the predominant opinion of theologians that theology is a practical rather than a theoretical discipline. It may be indeed a reflection upon knowledge, but the kind of knowledge that it is intent upon is necessary for our salvation, and not simply a group of items of information that may be true but make no difference to our lives beyond the acceptance of them. Virtually all the authors we shall examine are agreed on that thesis. How they *deal* with it is various. The things that we know in the pursuit of the life of faith are not verifiable hypotheses, like the laws of physics, or information, such as historical data, or conclusions drawn from inferences. Rather they involve an understanding of ourselves and our life, its failures, its satisfactions, its hopes, fears, affections, hatreds, and loves, including the endeavor to know ourselves well enough to be able to deal with our life. The knowledge of God, it is thought, is implicated in that self-knowledge: we cannot know ourselves properly unless we know God, and our knowledge of God, it is thought, is simultaneous with and involved in a knowledge and right ordering of ourselves and our lives.

Calvin drew attention to this practical matter of the knowledge of God right at the beginning of the *Institutes*. Indeed, it is not surprising that the Reformers, with their deep distrust of the independent reach of human reason, should support this practical view which preceded them. And so, for them, there is no knowledge of God that does not involve a right relationship with him, and there is no love of God that is not also repentance and a love of the neighbor. They expressed this for doctrinal purposes by saying, for example, that to know Christ is to know not the proper and correct doctrine of the Atonement or Incarnation, but to know him, as Melanchthon said in a famous phrase, by his benefits. Still, to know him by his benefits and also state a doctrine about it involves something like a statement that renders a true description, an assertion of these benefits, and how Christ brought them about. Luther, and later the Formula of Concord, repeatedly warned Christians against a merely historical or doctrinal faith, but at the same time there was no question in their minds that the faith was dependent on the historical events in the name of which it was preached. There was a kind of distinction *between* the rationale, order, or logic implicit in how one comes to believe and how one exercises belief on the one hand, *and* the logic appropriate to the belief one holds on the other, such that neither could be substituted for the other, and such that the two together in their mutual distinction were part of the articulation of the grammar of the faith. So Christian self-description for Protestants involved at one and the same time a set of belief assertions and a confidence that all Christian language, including those assertions, is self-involving language, and not neutral or informational language. The assurance that theology is a practical rather than a theoretical discipline did not settle this two-sidedness one way or the other. Assertions about practical knowledge are still assertions. And self-involving language, existential knowledge, remains in a kind of logical distinction to sheer assertions.

Later Protestant theology, the canon of the nineteenth and twentieth centuries, understood this dual aspect of Christian self-description as a problem. By and large it solved the problem by trying to make statements of belief functions of, or at least intelligible by reference to, a description of how we come to faith and how we exercise it. But there were always those who protested against this procedure by insisting on the objectivity of belief assertions, regardless of the fact that Christian faith is formed affectively rather than as a hypothesis. And so there came to be hot disputes about the priority of and logical relationship between the faith which is believed and the faith by which we believe. In that debate, one side would always try to make the concerns of the other a function of its own prior statement, neither denying some validity to the other. The anthropologist Clifford Geertz has suggested that

> sacred symbols function to synthesize a people's ethos—the tone, character, and quality of their life, its moral and aesthetic style and mood—and their world view—the picture they have of the way things in sheer actuality are, their most comprehensive ideas of order. In religious belief and practice, a group's ethos is rendered intellectually reasonable by being shown to represent a way of life ideally adapted to the actual state of affairs the world describes, while the world view is rendered emotionally convincing by being presented as an image of an actual state of affairs peculiarly well-arranged to accommodate such a way of life. . . . Religious symbols formulate a basic congruence between a particular style of life and specific (if, most often, implicit)

metaphysic, and in so doing sustain each with the borrowed authority of the other.[4]

Perhaps Geertz should have the final word on this matter; for him, the marvelous way that a religion has of functioning as a symbol system is not a problem at all but a miracle. Perhaps the very logic of the self-description of Christianity as a religion is that these two things don't *need* to be explained for their harmony. There is no need to explain, but only to describe them, distinctly and together. Still, in modern Protestant theology the debate over theology as, for example, either orthodox or existentialist, has become a distressing diversion. People on either side of the issue give priority to either Christian self-description or Christian theology as member of a class of disciplines. And also from either side one can show up as liberal or conservative.

The theological sorting out I propose to do will not, I am afraid, be very neat. (1) The basic issue will be how a representative of a type relates the two basic views of theology. But since Christianity is a specific religion, even for those who see it as philosophically grounded, a second question will be (2a) how a representative of a type relates specific *external* description of Christianity to Christian *self-description* on the one hand, and how he or she relates specific description of Christianity (2b) to a view of the general criteria for meaningful description on the other. As I stated earlier, the internal debate over the twofold character of Christian language—existential and/or objective— will enter obliquely.

4 ///////////////////////////// **Five Types**

of Theology ///////.

Type 1: Gordon Kaufman

In the first type that I am proposing, *theology as a philosophical discipline* in the academy takes complete priority over Christian self-description within the religious community called the Church, and Christian self-description, in its subordinate place, tends to emulate the philosophical character of academic theology by being as general as possible or as little specific about Christianity as it can be, and the distinction between external and internal description is basically unimportant. In Gordon Kaufman's monograph, *An Essay on Theological Method*, the task of the theologian is to search out the rules governing the use of the word or concept "God" as the organizing focus for a whole vocabulary. It is a metaphysical concept, the fruit not of information but of conceptual or imaginative construction. It is at least potentially universal as part of a quest for ultimate meaning, in the articulation of which the concepts "world" and "God" are correlative. Certainly it is in terms of these particular imaginative constructs that the three Western monotheistic faiths have construed the human quest. The concept "God" arises *formally* as ground and limit of the concept "world," and *materially* it arises out of the richness of human experience: for example, the experience of creativity, but also that of need and of desire. God must be the ultimate reference point for human cultural and moral concerns. The two functions of the concept "God" thus are the relativizing and the humanizing of the world. Since the concept "God" is not a report on information, and since the concepts that theology scrutinizes are employed to help us solve problems of meaningful moral and cultural living, theology is a practical rather than theoretical discipline. Still, it may be said to be theoretical in the sense that it argues a theoretical case—that is, adducing the underlying criteria of meaningfulness and universality that would justify the deployment of this type of concept, and testing any instance of it by those criteria. Theology is a philosophical enterprise resting on a set of statable, general criteria.

What about the status of the self-description of Christianity or of any specific religious tradition? First, the unit for specific description is for Kaufman both larger and smaller than Christianity, so that, properly speaking, there is no specific self-description of Christianity: the intelligible context enabling specific and ordinary language about God to function is "Western culture," though Kaufman does not tell us how that large, vague, and various hypostatization can be said to serve as a community that supports ordinary people with a common religious grammar. The concept of the culture as linguistic context here becomes so general and so intellectualized that it is robbed of all specificity. The ordinary user of the religious language of Western culture looks uncannily like an academic reader of histories of Western philosophy and theology with a stake in inventing a religious apologetic. The images or symbols of specific religious traditions become imaginative representations whose meaning is their paraphrasing (aptly or ineptly, and in the latter case they must be reformed) of the metaphysical, conceptual master construct. The aptness or ineptness of such images depends of course in large part on the cultural situation in which they arise.

The "ordinary language" meaning of "God" as a specific cultural construct of Western culture is ultimately indistinguishable from the general, metaphysical construct of the concept that is grounded presumably in the very structure of human nature and experience. If in this way the unit of specific description and self-description of a religious community is so large as to be only accidentally differentiated from humankind as a whole, there are, on the other hand, "sectarian" interpretations of God that are considerably smaller than, say, the unit "Christian religion." But they too "can no longer be regarded as autonomous and responsible only to their own private or idiosyncratic norms: They must come before the bar of the gradually emerging common discipline of theology."[1] Their talk about God and revelation has for its criterion of meaning its compatibility with the universal activity of the construction of the concept "God." Likewise implied is the priority of the "ordinary language" use of the accumulated cultural heritage over any special sectarian language.

In both respects—Christian theology as specific description or self-description of Christianity as a religion, and Christian theology as an academic discipline related to philosophy—Kaufman's essay represents a clear position. On the one hand, Christianity is given meaning by its inclusion in and contribution to a larger cultural heritage, so that "sectarian" self-description is accountable to—indeed, included in—external description. On the other hand, Christianity is one expression of a universal and inalienable human capacity or necessity. And just as there is no tension in principle within either of these two ways of doing theology, cultural and metaphysical, so there is none between them. There is no reason to think that there is a basic incompatibility between the monotheistic conceptualization of the quest for ultimate meaning and that of the religion of any other culture, such that the very terms in which we understand "religion" might have to be altered. In Kaufman's view, it seems, every specific religion is in principle as old as the creation, and its message is a republication of the natural and universal human quest. Theology is a philosophical discipline, and its endeavor to grapple with specific Christian description or self-description is not only subordinate to, but undertaken as part of, a general intellectual-cultural inquiry.

Type 2: David Tracy's Blessed Rage for Order

In type 2, theology is also a philosophical or academic discipline, but within that ordering, the specificity of Christian religion is taken very seriously, in a way in which external description and self-description merge into one, and the joint product is justified by a foundational philosophical scheme. David Tracy, in his book *Blessed Rage for Order*, looks for a revisionist, post-liberal, and post-neo-orthodox theology, fit for people in a postmodern situation, and says that such a theological model may be formulated as follows: "Contemporary Christian theology is best understood as philosophical reflection upon the meanings present in common human experience and the meanings present in the Christian tradition."[2]

There are separately statable, general, and fields-encompassing criteria for meaning (internal conceptual coherence), meaningfulness (language that discloses actual experience), and truth (transcendental or metaphysical explication of the condition of possibility of common human experience).[3] So theology is subject to judgment and evaluation by certain basic general criteria. But unlike Kaufman's essay, Tracy's signals an issue to be resolved. Theology is also explication of the Christian religion or the Christian "fact," which has a real specificity of its own and in its integrity has to be *correlated* to common human experience, the other source of theological reflection, for their mutual compatibility. And Tracy suggests that one should try to do better what Tillich tried to do in presenting correlatingly the Christian message as an answer to our culture's problems and its own secular answers to them. The issue, so far, is really one of compatibility between two apparently autonomous factors—a compatibility that is, at the outset at least, in question. The terms for that compatibility are those of experience. There is the immediately lived experience of a self that is obviously internal to itself and mediates this lived and preconceptual selfhood, both to itself and to the outside, by means of concepts, or, better, by means of symbols and metaphors that express and disclose that immediate self. Religious language is the indirect self-articulation of the prelinguistic, immediately experienced self. Obviously, when you want to talk about the meaningfulness of Christianity to such a self, it's got to be on those terms; otherwise no compatibility. You may have to say, "Sorry, no Christianity for me," but you'll have to say it formally by way of this kind of a general philosophical anthropology. In this view, the specificity of the Christian tradition is rendered not by *historical* description, as it was for nineteenth-century historians of dogma—F. C. Baur, for instance—which is only a preliminary task, nor by a kind of *social scientific* description, for which the Church would be the indispensable context in which the Christian symbol system alone can function properly. For a social scientist, the community is the field, or context, of the existential and conceptual interaction of its members, without which their common language would be inconceivable. Nothing like that for Tracy. For him the specific self-description of Christianity is one mode of a general description of religion, and that description is the work of phenomenology.

Phenomenology is the technical, reflective analysis, as it were from within, of the structure of distinctively human experience—in other words, of specific contents of human consciousness. It does not ask about the truth value of such experience, but simply asks what we sense as meanings in the world that becomes internalized within us. In turn, however, since there is a generic relationship between that world and the self that is open to it, the reverse is similarly the case.

Our experience in its immediacy as mediated externally is also our mode-of-being-in-the-world and not only the world's presence to us. Unlike the intellectual historian or historian of dogma for whom the historical essence is very hard to catch because it is always changing, phenomenological analysis supposes constant kinds of experience, even if their positive contents have to be articulated in all varying cultural terms. "Meanings" then are modes-of-being-in-the-world that are essences, or constant and identifiable characteristics, of the experiencing self. Hermeneutics is the formulation of principles for understanding such essences or modes-of-being-in-the-world through their articulation in discourse, particularly in the written texts that disclose them. There is a general structure presupposed in all intelligent exegesis, a kind of prescriptive rule that explains how it is possible for us to understand any and all discourse, especially texts.

The abstract scaffolding that Tracy applies for this purpose to any text is taken over from his mentor, Paul Ricoeur, especially from Ricoeur's subtle, dense, and beautiful little book, *Interpretation Theory*.[4] Every text has something called a meaning, and the meaning is first of all its semantic sense, but over and above that it is its referent. Ricoeur here makes use of a distinction first suggested by Gottlieb Frege. The sense of the text is its *what*, the referent is its *about what*, and together they make up the meaning of the text—what Ricoeur, using Edmund Husserl's language, calls the ideal or noematic meaning. It means simply that one is bound neither to the original situation in which the writing was produced, nor to the intention of the author, but that the text is now a fixed and stable quantity codified by means of the literary genre employed in experience of an extreme kind that Tracy calls a "limit experience," which can be either that of ecstasy or that of desperate crisis. Corresponding to such limit experiences is "limit language," the language in which such experience is disclosed. First-order religious language is not in the first place descriptive but expressive. *And* the trans-semantic referent—the extralinguistic referent, the *about what*—is just this: the lived experience, or mode-of-being-in-the-world, of an extreme limit to our lives. Perhaps it would be better to say that the languages invoke or evoke, rather than refer to, an extreme limit in our lives.

It happily turns out that the limit language and limit experience that form the religious dimension of our common human existence are also appropriate to the interpretation of the New Testament. It turns out, in effect, to nobody's particular surprise, that when we apply, after due argument about criteria of adequacy and appropriateness, the notions of limit experience and limit language to the New Testament, we find out that it is a religious book. It has a discernible and constant meaning. It is not simply a cultural amalgam that the historian of that period has to inform us about, nor is its meaning subject to the changing cultural situations of the readers. So what is the meaning that the New Testament's limit language discloses? The ordinary is transgressed and a new and extraordinary but possible mode-of-being-in-the-world is disclosed. "As parabolic that language redescribes our experience in such manner that the sense of its meaning (its now limit-metaphor) discloses a limit referent which projects and promises that one can in fact live a life of wholeness, of total commitment, or radical honesty and agapic love in the presence of the gracious God of Jesus the Christ."[5]

Now, what have we heard about theology? Clearly it is not basically, though perhaps at a secondary level, Christian self-description. First, theology is fundamentally an academic, philosophical discipline, both for the formal and universally applicable, context-invariant criteria by which it is governed, and for the transcendental or metaphysical condition of possibility on which the experience-anthropology rests.

Second, there is no cutting difference between external description and Christian self-description, largely because the context for both is the "meaning" structure supplied by the notion of the self as consciousness and by the phenomenological procedure that analyzes it. Meaning, as the internal experience of selves, and religious experience in particular, is the glue that allows external and internal description to be one, and Christian description or self-description is one instance of the general class "religious meaningfulness." That class, again, is a universal anthropological phenomenon, philosophically grounded. From another view, however, there is a very large distance between Christian self-description and phenomenological description of Christianity. If the social, linguistic community is the necessary condition or context for having a common self-description, we have a very different relation between external and self-description and one for which meaning as religious experience—whatever its status—is simply not part of the grammar. It is interesting that the Church as the necessary context for the use of Christian concepts and language plays no part at all in Tracy's layout of his method. *Experience* is its substitute. Finally, if Kaufman tended to be general in his specific description of Christianity—it's an aspect of Western cultural history—Tracy is even more so: Christianity is one mode of consciousness under the auspices of a philosophical anthropology.

But doesn't Tracy, unlike Kaufman, see a need for correlating, if not specific external description and specific Christian self-description, or the two types of theology, philosophical theology and self-description of the community, then at least the meanings presented in the common religious experience and those of the Christian tradition? Yes, and there is a not easily locatable but tangible difference between the two men. Perhaps phenomenological method elucidating consciousness can see culturally and historically separated forms of consciousness better, each in its particularity, than a kind of rationalism in which every specific, culturally conditioned religious image is, if not equally, at least more or less gray. (In contrast, Kaufman's rationalism is something of a relief after Tracy's tortuous procedure for making publicly and universally accessible supposed human realities that remain elusive and in doubt, except for those already persuaded. For some people, "religion" is a disposition and a way of life rather than an experience located deep inside the self.) But finally the correlation is a matter of subsuming the specifically Christian under the general, experiential religious, as one "regional" aspect.

Type 3: Friedrich Schleiermacher

We turn to type 3, but we have it only in an ambiguous form because its greatest representative may not fit it. Of all modern theologians, Friedrich Schleiermacher raises perhaps most acutely the issue of the relation between the two kinds of theology that we have discussed. But he does it in an interesting form. He has often been represented as giving us a complex, confusing, and possibly reductionist outlook on the relationship between philosophy and theology. I contend that this is not the case. There is very little doubt that on this matter he stands at a far remove from both the types represented by Gordon Kaufman and David Tracy. For both of them, theology is unequivocally in the first place a philosophical discipline rather than specifically Christian self-description undertaken in the Church. But if the choice were between these two kinds of outlooks, Schleiermacher would not—indeed, he did not—hesitate for even a moment. Theology was an academic discipline indeed, but he had no doubt that it was *at least* equally and quite independently Christian self-description within the religious community called the Church. He makes this clear right at the beginning of his short *Outline of Theology*, and at the very beginning, in the second paragraph, of his classic work, *The Christian Faith*. Is theology more one than the other? In any case, it is a discipline in which the two, academic method and Christian self-description, are correlated as two autonomous yet reciprocally related factors. But in fact we should go further than that. Even if one assigns theology to academic study, it is definitely *not* philosophy that is its primary home. Theology is not a philosophical discipline for Schleiermacher. The real question for Schleiermacher is, rather, whether Christian self-description is completely autonomous, or whether it bears some re-semblance—and if so, how strong or of what kind—to external de-scriptions of it as a specific religion. The issue of philosophy is secondary, because Schleiermacher treats it as important only to the extent that philosophy plays a role in defining the criteria to which the "cultural sciences" must be subject.

Schleiermacher thinks of theology as second-order didactic language that must be conceptually precise; but *first-order* Christian language is not conceptually precise at all. It is expressive of the Christian religious relationship to God. Theology is second-order reflection on what Schleiermacher calls *Glaubensaussagen*: first-order statements that are themselves internal expressions of the wedding of a universal human condition (religion, or the feeling of absolute dependence), with a specific "positive" or cultural form which provides the only way in which such a condition can be present. In the case of Christianity, the feeling of absolute dependence becomes a matter of referring every-thing in that feeling "to the redemption accomplished by Jesus of Nazareth."[6] If we ask which view of theology has priority for Schleier-macher, theology as academic discipline or specific Christian self-description in the service of the Church, there is no doubt of his answer. It is not that theology is not an academic discipline for him. But it is not an academic discipline that is in any way in conflict with theology as autonomous and second-order self-description of the Christian Church.

The real question for Schleiermacher is, How is Christian self-description related to external descriptions of Christianity? To answer it, he borrows what he calls a series of propositions from what he calls

Ethics, which is really the study of culture, humanistic or social-scientific, and Philosophy of Religion, which is really a comparative study of types of religion, and Apologetics, which is really a study of what he regards as the specific Essence of Christianity. "Essence" here is the point at which internal and external descriptions of Christianity come together. Because they join he calls it Apologetics, and yet he proposes that what he says under that rubric is really only borrowed from it. In other words, he leads you more and more toward a place where you will replicate, as it were from your own inside or by placing yourself within the conspectus of religious life, what *he* has been saying to you as a kind of didactic specialist.

Does he succeed? I'm not sure. His method is a bit like Tracy's, but much more restrained and indirect, allowing your own internal experience to make the important moves. He has tried to give you the *location* of Christian self-description. It is in Christian self-consciousness, in experience, but experience that for him takes place within a broader experience structure called not meaning or religion but the Church. Then he moves back and asks: If experience is a ground on which all Christian self-description in the Church stands, how is language related to it? Again, he describes a kind of succession of developments, from a kind of first-order language to a final and rel-atively frozen didactic form of that language, which is Doctrine, and which is never more than a temporary expression for one's own times. All along Schleiermacher is giving you something that might be called a phenomenological account, an inquiry into a specific form or expres-sion of immediate self-consciousness. Compared to what goes under the name of phenomenology later on, this one is mercifully home-grown, to use a felicitous expression of Stephen Crites's. It does not have any very high-flown philosophical auspices for Schleiermacher, at least not so far as he is aware. All you need, he says, is a little introspection. He is simply suggesting what he thinks is a proper inside view of what it is to be human, one that all of us, if only we looked in on the real ground of ourselves, would be aware of. If Christian statements are to make sense, they do so by their bearing on the specific changes in our experience that are represented by Christian terms, especially, Sin and Redemption, which is the Christian's most basically experienced antithesis. It is clear to Schleiermacher, as he said in two very long published letters to a friend when he was getting the second edition of his *Christian Faith* ready,[7] that Christian use of language always remains distinctive and irreducible to any other, even if its home lies in experience. As I said, he saw no contradictions between broadly human experience and a relatively closed religious communion which "forms an ever self-renewing circulation of the religious self-consciousness within certain definite limits, and a propagation of the religious emotions arranged and organized within the same limits, so that there can be some kind of definite understanding as to which individuals belong to it and which do not."[8] And this we call a Church.

So the language of a Church is always community-specific and can never be dissolved, as Gordon Kaufman proposes, into a more general cultural or, for that matter, a philosophical-technical vocabulary. There is, then, a kind of informal transition from external description to a very clear sense of internal self-description. The two are autonomous of each other, yet reciprocally related or correlated, and phenomenology is the discipline that shows they really belong together. Schleiermacher, however, clearly indicates that though all dogmatic propositions are descriptions of human states, that is, of self-consciousness, and that his is the basic form of dogmatic utterance, the description, moving from outside to inside, of the location of Christian discourse still is not identical with doctrine itself. Again, in the long letter just referred to, Schleiermacher insists that in the introduction to *The Christian Faith*, when he describes the place of Christianity and Christian doctrines within human consciousness, he is making no dogmatic statements. Phenomenology and doctrinal content are correlated, but to talk of their identity would be inappropriate. This is a far cry from David Tracy, for whom it seems to be the case that Christian "meanings" may be fairly represented as one specific mode of general religious consciousness.

There can be no doubt, however, that internal and external descriptions of Christianity are positively or harmoniously related, so that in that respect there can be no conflict between theology as Church discipline and theology as academic discipline. The same positive relation holds for Schleiermacher between theology and other specific disciplines, especially history and the natural sciences. In contrast to Hegel, he has no supertheory or system by which to mediate between religion-neutral historical descriptions and Christian religious descriptions of the same events, so he tries to correlate directly, each from its own autonomous base, a historical reading of the Christology of the Gospels and a religious reading of the experience of religious redemption in

Christ. General agreement among commentators ever since his day has been that he failed at nothing more succinctly than this attempt. But still it is clear what the direction of the endeavor was. Similarly with the relation between theology and philosophy. Theology is not founded on philosophy. The two are quite autonomous. Schleiermacher thinks that both moral philosophy and metaphysical philosophy lead to an idea of a transcendent ground of all being and action. But like Kant, he also believes that this inevitable idea never becomes an item for real knowledge. But we are immediately related to that same ground that is elsewhere elusive, in the experience or immediate self-consciousness of ourselves as absolutely dependent, which is the heart of religion. Thus, there is a real reciprocal relationship between philosophy and theology. At the same time, Schleiermacher insisted on the autonomy of theology from philosophy, which cannot serve as a foundational discipline for theology.

In sum, then, Schleiermacher, unlike our previous two exhibits, does not give priority to academic or philosophical theology, nor does he make philosophy the basis of theology. Furthermore, he insists that fundamental theology—the introduction to *The Christian Faith*—is not a part of the dogmatic enterprise. But neither is it a philosophical enterprise. Theology as academic enterprise and as Christian self-description in the Church must be correlated. Philosophy and theology must be correlated. External and self-description of Christianity must be correlated, and in each case, two factors are autonomous yet reciprocally related, but that reciprocity and mutual autonomy is not explained by any more basic structure of thought under which the two factors would be included.

Type 4: Karl Barth

The representative I've chosen for type 4 insists even more unequivocally than does Schleiermacher that Christianity has its own distinctive language, which is not to be interpreted without residue into other ways of thinking and speaking. Unlike Schleiermacher, Karl Barth is absolutely certain that the meaning of Christian statements is not their reference, a modification of immediate self-consciousness. It is clear at the outset that theology as critical Christian self-reflection or self-description not only has priority over theology as an academic discipline, but that this priority is to be taken in two ways. First, theology is not philosophically founded, and, second, what makes theology an orderly and systematic procedure (the Germans use the word *science* to cover not only the natural sciences but every systematic procedure, including theology) is for Barth not a set of universal, formal criteria which are certain and all-fields-encompassing and can therefore be stated apart from the context of specific application. In that highly formal sense also, and not only in the sense that Barth has no philosophical anthropology or metaphysics into which to fit theology, the way Tracy and Kaufman do, theology is not philosophically grounded for him. But in addition, in that theology has its own rules of what makes it a science—a set of rules that are usually implicit and developed only as the context of theology itself develops—in that sense also Christian self-description is quite independent of every external endeavor to describe Christianity as a specific religion: for example, every historical account. Theology is Christian self-description first, and the only question is whether theology in this sense subordinates or eliminates all relation to the other enterprise, both philosophical and specific external description. Barth leaves absolutely no doubt that for him, unlike Schleiermacher, fundamental theology—or, as he calls it, Prolegomena—is internal to, part of, the dogmatic enterprise. It is not a procedure for correlating theology to other disciplines in the academic spectrum.

If there is a reductionism here, it goes in the opposite direction to that of Kaufman and Tracy. On the very first page of the very first volume of his enormous *Church Dogmatics*, Barth tells us that theology is a function of the Church; specifically, it arises because the Church is accountable to God for its discourse about God.[9] To the best of its lights, then, the Church must undertake a critique and correction of her discourse in the light of the norm she sees as the presence of God to the Church, in obedience to God's grace. Expanding the concept of the Church in a manner typical of him, Barth says that the criterion of Christian discourse is the being of the Church, and the being of the Church for him is Jesus Christ, God in his presence or turning to humanity. The question is, Does Christian discourse come from him and move toward him, and is it in accordance with him?

Note one interesting implication: First-person direct address *to* God, speaking and acting in his presence, and talk or discourse *about* God are presumably not nearly so sharply distinguishable as they are for some other theologians. And if one pushes this same line of thought, it is most likely that, for Barth, first-order discourse or first-order theology and second-order discourse or theology will not finally be as sharply distinguishable as they are for most others. It is not that such a distinction as that between self-involving statements and the analysis of self-involving statements—language about Christianity and Christian language use—is not part of Barth's vocabulary. But it obviously seems to him that such rules, even a rule as formal as this, must be ad hoc. It must depend on the specific context in which one speaks; it cannot be context-invariant. I suspect he would say that even in regard to intertheological talk—even within theological discourse—it depends on what issues one addresses, whether this distinction should or should not be kept. Barth would want to affirm that in actual practice it may from time to time have to be violated.

Theology as specific and critical Christian self-description and self-examination by the Church of its language takes absolute priority over theology as an academic discipline. Philosophy as conceptual system describing and referring to "reality" is not a basis on which to build theology, and even philosophy as a set of formal, universal rules or criteria for what may count as coherent and true in Christian discourse as in every other kind of conceptual practice is not basic to or foundational of Christian theology. He would, I suspect, not object at all to Schleiermacher's indirect and maieutic guidance of the reader in the introduction to *The Christian Faith*, from external placement of Christian discourse whether in a more general or more specific context, to the location for internal self-description. But he would chide Schleiermacher if Schleiermacher made his description of that self-description subject to an invariant, formal, universal criterion: *the* test for the meaningfulness and coherence of dogmatic assertions is their referring only by way of a co-reference to experience of absolute dependence. The rule that only that kind of language is meaningfully Christian which is a report on a self-expression in symbolic form of faith as experience, or even the rule that all Christian language is self-involving language, is externally imposed; it implies a general theory of the meaningfulness of Christian language, and Barth doesn't want that any more than he wants any other general theory as indispensable condition for the possibility of making sense of theology.

But even though formal rules or criteria for coherence, meaningfulness, and truth are context-dependent, one cannot use human language without *some* such formal guidance as that. Barth is well aware that the tradition since the Reformation, and more specifically since the nineteenth century, has distinguished very sharply between two genres within Christian discourse, even while trying to unify them. On the one hand, there is the sort of discourse that appears to be cognitive in character, in that it gives descriptions that refer to an actually true state of affairs, "reality." Faith takes the form of dogmatic assertions, even though this use of Christian language is not backed by a general theory of reference-making or truth-speaking, or of concepts as descriptions. But Barth is fully persuaded that we cannot do without some such formal categories and categorical distinctions as those between meaning and truth, sense and reference, description and explanation. In this highly formal sense, acknowledging the need for formal rules and criteria, but letting their use be governed by the specific theological issue at hand, and by the general rule that absolute priority be given to Christian theology as Christian self-description within the religious community called the Church, or the Christian community, Barth acknowledges the need for a formal or technical philosophical vocabulary in theology. If theology in that criteriological sense can be firmly governed by theology, one need not fear a second use or understanding of philosophy within theology.

One not only can but must make use of technical philosophical schemes of a metaphysical sort in the process of using Christian language in its descriptive or assertive mode. But once again the rule is that that language must be highly formal, in the sense that the use of the conceptual scheme must be firmly governed by the specific Christian descriptions that such schemes are asked to render in second-order re-descriptions. This subordinate use of philosophy in theology receives no systematic explanation. Barth has no supertheory, say, like that of David Tracy, for assigning Christian meaning to a more general context, and therefore assigning it its place within that context. The subordinating assignment is made unsystematically or asymptotically. How it is done is a matter of seeing the application in a given context. In his book on Anselm's ontological argument for the existence of God, Barth makes much more explicit use of a conceptual scheme that borrows from medieval realism, and in his exposition of the doctrine of justification by faith, such concepts are much more implicit. One cannot unite the rules for proper use of philosophy in theology into a system, but lack of system is not the same as inconsistency.

Barth is clearly aware that there is another equally if not more important aspect of Christian language, one that should not conflict with the subordinate role of philosophy in theology just described: that is, that all Christian language is self-involving, existential; that whether it is directed toward God or the neighbor, it is the learning and exercising of concepts in a performative manner. To learn, for example, to explicate Christian scripture about faith, hope, and love, is not only to master these concepts, but to be able to apply them pertinently and propose the same to others. On the one hand, justification by faith is a doctrine that functions as a rule in, let us say, orthodox Christian discourse. Not only does it function as a rule but it looks as though it were asserting something about how God deals with human beings, and to that extent is a statement that holds true regardless of the attitude of the person or persons articulating it. On the other hand, it is equally true that the assertion works as a concept that is meaningless apart from the appropriate attitude of gratitude, and obedience subsequent to gratitude, which is the condition for understanding it— indeed, the manner in which it is understood. But here again, Barth's view, at least implicitly, is not to apply universal criteria for the meaningfulness of Christian statements or Christian concepts. They work this way, as self-involving statements, but that does not mean that if this rule applies, then the previous rules for description and assertion do not apply. The point is so to subordinate the rules to the actual use of the language that one will not be tempted to prescribe rules for it but allow the rules to be fragmentary if that is what the proper and consistent use of the language seems to imply. There can be for Barth no single, articulable, super-rule for the way in which Christian language is used. He seems to be performing a balancing act, carrying on his tightrope the nineteenth- and twentieth-century canon of Protestant theology texts, one kind on each shoulder.

Philosophy, thus, is not excluded from theology but firmly subordinate to theology as normed Christian self-description or critical self-examination by the Church of her language concerning God, in God's presence. Although the rule for that subordination cannot be stated abstractly but must be worked in specific application, Barth is so rigorously consistent about it that he even regards any *principled* priority choice between describing faith statements as either existential or objective, as a philosophical rather than a theological decision—and therefore will not make it. However, throughout his dogmatic enterprise, he has made a *pragmatic* priority choice: In view of what he judges the theological *situation* of his day to be, the descriptive—if you will, objective—enterprise must be given priority. If Christian theologians put forth truth claims but cannot put them into a specific class of assertions—they are certainly not hypotheses to be demonstrated or verified—they must above all insist on the integrity or irreducibility of Christian language as a form of description. The language of grace, predestination, redemption, sin, and so on must, in order to be descriptive, have an internal coherence that distinguishes it from its equally necessary application to other linguistic contexts, such as that of our practical life in Church and world.

In other words, the situation of the Church, or Christian life in our culture in our day, is such that Christian subjectivity, or how to become a Christian, must be—not existentially, but theologically—subordinate to the *what* of Christianity. The logic of faith, which takes Christian doctrinal discourse as an internally coherent, irreducible language form, is not only distinct from the logic of coming to and exercising faith as trust, but takes pragmatic priority over the latter. Again, not in Christian life, but in the present theological task. And yet the two belong together fully—that is part of the logic or grammar of the faith. But the grammatical *rule* cannot be a rule that would state prescriptively or in the abstract how self-involving discourse and normative description without reference to self-involvement are one; that we cannot do. Yet, Barth insists, do not call it a paradox, a principled violation of the criterion of noncontradiction supposedly acceptable on a loftier plane. No, the internal coherence of the two modes of discourse is fragmentary; its fullness as the logos or rationale of faith, hidden but not absent.

Barth thus finds the heart of theological discourse in the constant transition between first-order Christian statements, especially biblical confession and exegesis, and their second-order redescription, in which description as internal dogmatic description makes use of third-order free, unsystematic, and constant reference to conceptual patterns of a non-Christian, nontheological kind—including phenomenology, conceptual analysis, Hegelian philosophy, analyses of contemporary culture, and so on. But the governance of the third is from the side of the transition between first- and second-order discourse, and therefore the flow of interpretation moves in *that* direction, in contrast to the flow of interpretation for Tracy, for whom the meaning of Christian statements is their anthropological or experiential reference, and in contrast to Schleiermacher, for whom the matter remains one of correlation and ambiguity.

I wish to propose that the meaning of the "literal sense" in biblical reading is more nearly embodied in this kind of procedure or outlook than in the others we have examined. It says that among other uses or capacities to use a text Christianly which go into a Christian understanding of a text, there is a *descriptive* use—more appropriate to some texts than to others. And *if* one speaks in terms of "reference" to a subject matter described—a complex, perhaps confused, perhaps indispensable way of speaking—then there is not a *split* reference to the described subject matter. The text means what it says, and so the reader's redescription is just that, a redescription and not the discovery of the text as symbolic representation of something else more profound. But in the *process* of redescription we can—and indeed cannot do other than—employ our own thought structures, experiences, conceptual schemes; there is neither an explicit mode for showing how to *correlate* these things with the job of redescription, nor is there a fundamental conflict between them. Without knowing success or lack of it in any given case beforehand, it is an article of faith that it *can* be done; it *is* done. Barth goes as far, I believe, as one can in articulating the largely implicit logic governing the sensus literalis. It is of a piece with his general theological outlook. If one is interested in the sensus literalis, his theology represents the type with which it is most nearly congruent.

A word about the relationship between Christian self-description and external description, trying to do justice to the specificity of the Christian religion, is now in order. Obviously, it does not have for Barth the character of mutual autonomy and reciprocity that Schleiermacher, for example, assigns to them systematically: as when he stresses the need for a notion of miracle in Christianity that will be genuinely Christian but will also be compatible with a notion of novelty arrived at independently by a physical and biological cosmology. Barth would agree with the autonomy of the two disciplines, Christian self-description and specific external description of Christianity, provided that it were always held to be provisional and not the fruit of absolutely systematic distinction and correlation. Barth is skeptical, though not dogmatically skeptical, about any universal *Wissenschaftsbegriff*. Certainly it does not include theological method (that would be too philosophical), but he wonders to what extent it includes physical, natural, social, and human sciences across the board. This in fact was his dispute in 1931 with his philosophical colleague and friend, Heinrich Scholz, who had adduced a set of postulates on the basis of which to judge whether any given procedure can lay claim to "scientific" status: the proposition postulate, coherence postulate, controllability postulate, congruity postulate.[10] Even the first of these, the law of noncontradiction, is acceptable in theology only within limits that are undoubtedly difficult for a general theoretician, Barth says. Instead of this set within which he picks and chooses, he sets down the criterion of what he calls appropriateness to the subject matter; in other words, the criterion must be rules governed by the context and not imposed on it. He claims that for theology there is no such thing as a general context-invariant criteriology, certainly in contrast to liberals like Kaufman and Tracy and conservatives like Henry and perhaps parts of Schleiermacher. If in the process of this assertion of criteria for a knowledge appropriate to the subject matter or object, Barth sounds like a traditional metaphysician who wants to make *theological* information do service for what in the eighteenth century used to be the duty of school metaphysics—to tell us about the realities of God, world, and soul corresponding to our ideas of them—the impression is misleading. Barth simply had not had the privilege of visiting the classrooms in which Anglo-Saxon philosophy of language and French theories of semiotics and semantics are taught. He is indeed talking about knowledge appropriate to reality, but there is no theory of reality and no theory of classes of assertions involved. Neither is there any across-the-board rejection of other specific methods or "sciences," especially if they sit loose to the application of general all-fields-encompassing criteria to their own procedures.

The final result is that prolegomena to dogmatics is not the foundation of dogmatics either by a conceptual philosophical scheme or by formal philosophical criteria or by the aid of some specific Christianity-describing discipline such as, for example, historical criticism, which would underwrite the possibility or conceivability of Christian discourse. Instead, prolegomena to dogmatics is part of dogmatics itself; it attempts insofar as is possible—and it is a limited matter indeed— to exhibit the rules or fragments of rules implicit in the ruled use of language which is the sign system of the sociolinguistic community called the Church. One can therefore designate no relationship *in prin-*

ciple between external descriptions of Christianity and Christian self-description, but one must not exclude as a matter of principle the possibility of overlap at specific, possibly even mutually contradictable, points of actual investigation. Similarly, there is no reason there cannot be a friendly, mutual delimitation of territory between specific studies of a general topic, such as anthropology, from the side of the more-or-less exact sciences (Barth has in mind biology in particular) on the one hand, and a theological study of human phenomena on the other. Provided only that neither description impinges on the other by asking the other to adopt what functions as explanatory hypothesis on its own ground. In one case, Barth actually came as close as anybody in his generation and in his geographical area to discovering a specific mode of studying Scripture in which external and internal Christian description converge: literary study of a certain kind of biblical narrative is a distinct mode that may or may not overlap with historical study but is certainly logically distinct from historical study, and it bears a strong family resemblance to theological exegesis, especially of the kind employing the literal sense.

The relationship between internal self-description and external description thus remains ad hoc, with freedom for each side, possible family resemblance, and obedience to the criterion of the priority of Christian self-description as the task of the Church.

Type 5: D. Z. Phillips

From a theology of correlation that may or may not ground Christian self-description and external description in a covering theory for both (the former case corresponding to type 2; the latter, to type 3, if Schleiermacher fits it rather than the type 2), and from a view that subordinates external description to Christian self-description and denies both philosophical foundations to theology, although admitting to philosophy a role governed by Christian self-description, we turn to our final and fifth type as Christian self-description with no holds barred. There is not even a subordinated place for philosophy within theology, neither in adducing criteria for coherence, adequacy, or appropriateness, nor most certainly in the employment, either materially or formally, of any metaphysical scheme by the theologian. "It has been far too readily assumed that dispute between the believer and the unbeliever is over a *matter of fact*. Philosophical reflection on the reality of God then becomes the philosophical reflection appropriate to an assertion of a matter of fact. . . . this is a misrepresentation of the religious concept. . . . philosophy can claim justifiably to show what is meaningful in religion only if it is prepared to examine religious concepts in the contexts from which they derive their meaning."[11]

D. Z. Phillips, who writes these words in an essay entitled, "Faith, Scepticism, and Religious Understanding," rightly—that is to say, consistently—also says on behalf of the religious believer, " 'You say that when applied to God words such as "exists," "love," "will," etc., do not mean what they signify in certain non-religious contexts. I agree. You conclude from this that religion is meaningless, whereas the truth is that you are failing to grasp the meaning religion has.' "[12] Why this misunderstanding? It won't do to talk about God as though he were an additional fact among all the others that we can either adduce or cross out. "It makes as little sense to say God's existence is not a fact as it does to say God's existence is a fact."[13] The error, according to Phillips, is grammatical; when we say that something is a fact we indicate not a description of that something but its context: that is, what it would and would not be sensible to say or do in connection with it. But this is not the grammar of the concept of divine reality. Phillips suggests that the appropriate question with regard to the comparison between "God" as concept and descriptions of fact is not, Are they both real? but What kind of reality is the reality of physical objects and what kind of reality is the reality of "God"?[14] To ask a question about the reality of God is to ask a question about a kind of reality, not about the reality of this or that, in much the same way as asking about the reality of physical objects is not to ask about the reality of this or that physical object. But asking that kind of question is asking for criteria. How do you judge whether or not you've got the right grammar? How do you judge, how do you know, what kind of talk concerning religion is meaningless and what is meaningful or appropriate? Answer: Not from the outside! You know, you judge by doing, by using the concepts, and using them within their own context, which is how concepts always work. In this case, using the concepts means using them in the specific religious tradition, so that even conflicts over the reality of God are conflicts between differing religions' use of the word. It would be a conflict over the functioning of "Yahweh" and "Allah," not over the factuality of someone designated by either term. "Theology can claim justifiably to show what is meaningful in religion only when it has an internal relation to religious discourse. Philosophy can make the same claim only if it is prepared to examine religious concepts in the contexts from which they derive their meaning."[15]

We noted earlier that certain theologians who also give priority to Christian theology as Christian self-description (for example, Barth) might be making the same kinds of distinctions. There are first-order theological statements of belief and confession. There are second-order statements examining or reflecting on these first-order statements in the context of the discourse itself—that is, within a Christian context. And then there are third-order statements that clarify or show us why or how it is the case that statements within a religious context are not the same as apparently similar or identical statements made outside the religious contexts. But for theologians like Barth, these distinctions are not absolute rules but essential guides or signposts for orientation. They would say that we must be prepared in actual practice to make transitions, to slide from one mode to another in connective ways, but for this operation our distinctions don't make provision. But D. Z. Phillips is made of sterner stuff than that. For him, the rule of inside and outside talk concerning religion is absolute, and theology is strictly inside talk, though he is not so clear about whether (and when) it is first- or second-order talk. Phillips quotes Peter Winch approvingly: "One cannot apply criteria of logic to modes of social life as such. For instance, science is one such mode and religion is another; and each has criteria of intelligibility peculiar to itself."[16] If theology is internal to the religion itself, how do you adjudicate between conflicting claims or descriptions? Phillips has two sorts of answers. One is a claim to authority. If you are talking within a conceptual or linguistic system, you owe fealty to normative instances of it, even if you do not want to specify one of them as more normative than the whole in all its complexity together. The other answer is a rule that distinguishes the logic of science and formulation of its principles from theology. In the latter, unlike the former, there has to be a personal element. "The foundation of a theological system is based on the non-formalized theology which is within the religious way of life carried on by the person who is constructing a theological system."[17] Surely the two procedures, that of systematizing and that of nonformal religious theologizing, are compatible. Theologians who are rightly pursuing their craft are those who have internalized the concepts of their religious community, so that their use of them is at the same time their performance of the capacities that those concepts describe. "The systematic theology is a sophistication of that theology which is necessarily present in so far as religious language is present."[18] The two things ought not to be taken separately. Authority, if it plays any role for Phillips's "inside" view at all, is not to be taken as a principle for right knowledge. It is rather an aid in finding one's way in territory that, even when familiar, still always has to be learned; nurture for a capacity that is exercised conceptually as well as existentially. But does Phillips in fact succeed in giving us signposts for keeping "systematic" and "nonformal religious theology," first- and second-order theology, both together and yet distinct? I think not; and the outcome is a muddle in which it is difficult to distinguish between second-order theology and philosophy, and between at least some aspects of first-order theology and completely esoteric talk.

For Phillips, "theology" is internal to religion, and the distinction between inside and outside is, at least at first glance, clear and sharp. "The criteria of what can sensibly be said of God are to be found *within* the religious tradition."[19] The unreality of God, he tells us, does not occur *within* a religion but between religions, and he gives a telling example, which may well be assuming a renewed urgency in our day. How did Paul know that the God he worshiped was also the God of Abraham? It was by asserting that both stood within a common religious tradition. How do you adjudicate *that* assertion? Finally, I suspect, Phillips would say, by an appeal to authority, the authority of the book. But in this case, "authority" would probably refer to the "plain" reading of the so-called prophecies in the text or to a generic continuity between plain and figural reading. But "authority" is not any one isolated case of itself, such as the contexts of half of one half-shared text; it is the tradition at large, much like what a social anthropologist might call a "culture," or "structures of significance or established codes"—in other words, a specific social language that is ruled by conventions, an informally coherent sign system for which the question of what it is *about* or what it refers to is an internal matter. To outside observers, be they philosophers or social scientists, the language ought to be about itself—unless, that is, they are confused by philosophical or scientific "methods" that crave universal criteria for meaning and truth, logics that are then prescribed to every language game right across the board. And to Phillips's sorrow, the number of such confused people is endless, and their mistake is curious: It is the sort of error where one does not say to the person, "Well, we disagree, don't we?" and like all arguments there's an end to it somewhere, because no different examples and no further reasons can be adduced. Phillips, rather, *seems* to be saying, "If you don't agree with me, you don't understand what I'm saying, you're confused."

The most common form this confusion takes among philosophers—not social scientists, who are, if anything, a yet more invidiously confused lot—is that God is taken to be one more fact, and therefore a member of that class of reality. "The reality of God is made subject to wider criteria of intelligibility. Like the particular hypotheses about the distance of the sun from the earth, the profit in business, or the existence of unicorns, beliefs about God are thought to have a relative reality—that is, the reality of the hypothesis which is relative to the hypothesis by which it is assessed."[20] This confusion, he says, following Wittgenstein, is largely due to a prejudice, the philosophical craving for generality, "That what constitutes an intelligible move in one context must constitute an intelligible move in *all* contexts."[21]

Phillips would have a lot of philosophical company today, but not nearly all of it as friendly to the cause of religion as he might like. Richard Rorty agrees that truth and certainty must be spelled with lowercase instead of uppercase letters and must be found out variously, case by case, but he thinks they may become part of a kind of informal, large-scale, and ongoing conversation, which is what serious thought is all about and the nearest we can come to having a unitary cultural and intellectual context. In that conversation, he says, religion is by now simply a kind of atrophied subconversation that has its own rules and so can't be faulted on grounds of internal coherence, but it just isn't where things are at these days. Religion is empty with regard to any larger connections. Deciding for or against it isn't very momentous. Alasdair MacIntyre tends to agree with Rorty but for opposite reasons. For him, religion is unbelievable because in the social and therefore linguistic contexts of our day and time, it is not a way for investing your moral passions significantly, whereas for Rorty investing moral passions in anything is a rather vulgar, confused, and undesirable thing to do. Two opposite philosophical ways to skin the same religious cat.

Summing up so far. Completely unlike Kaufman and Tracy, Phillips thinks that the business of philosophy is to clarify the complete distinctiveness of religion (and of theology as part of religion), in this case Christianity, so that theology is seen to be completely a matter of Christian self-description. Theology, in turn, is responsible to the Christian community or tradition and seeks to exhibit, even as it is responsible to, the informal rules that constitute the common Christian language context. Responsible to what? That is perhaps a complex matter, for it is not anything in particular that represents the tradition so as to function authoritatively—and this for a particular reason to which we shall return.

In the meantime, philosophy does not remain subordinate within theology—as for Barth, with whom Phillips's position otherwise has some things in common—but wholly external; more drastically external than was the case for Schleiermacher, for whom the mutual autonomy of the two involved a degree of reciprocity. "External" it remains in its two forms: first, as what the Germans call Wissenschaftslehre and we earlier called criteriology—that is, a network of fields-encompassing or universal rules that become the measure by which to judge whether any specific set of concepts and discourse is coherent and meaningful. For Phillips there is no such set of rules external to a specific context itself. In large part, Barth would agree as thoroughly as Kaufman and Tracy would disagree. But Barth would qualify his agreement in one respect. He would always see it as provisional: there might be enough overlap among contexts to allow limited overlap between logics or criteria. That fact in turn would clue us in on the proviso, important for Barth, that this kind of overlap might mean that criteria—for example, of coherence and noncontradiction—are fields-encompassing in God's eyes, though not in ours, and that the declaration *in principle* that they are not and cannot be is therefore too *prescriptive* a rule. I believe that Phillips comes close to that kind of prescriptive stance. If he is actually *being* prescriptive (and I'm not saying he is: often the specific examples are the meat of his own case, which is nice, but sometimes the generalization sticks out well before the example gets going), I would be in an ironic situation, for we would in that case have the most drastic and purist assertion that theology is Christian self-description taking the shape of a prescriptive *philosophical* argument and theory, which would mean that the two extreme end positions of this typology would meet, like a snake curled in on itself. Such an outcome would only prove how silly it was to start this enterprise in the first place. I therefore have an emotional investment in Phillips's *not* doing what I fear he might be doing. And that's why I also hope that he might agree at some stage that those who don't agree with him completely on this matter of logic and the logic of belief might actually be disagreeing with him rather than being simply confused and lacking in understanding. For complete theoretic certainty tends in these theologically chastened days to be more often a philosophical than a theological stance.

Second, of course, philosophy—not only as foundational criteriology but even more as speculative scheme, especially as anthropological or metaphysical scheme—is out of bounds for theology, and this for both philosophical and theological reasons. General theories about human beings miss the point in any case; one could cite the notion of characterizing human beings as internal containers of consciousness, experience, and a single process called understanding, apart from specific things understood, as typical of such misplaced generalizations. As for metaphysical schemes, it is philosophically wrong to think of God as one more fact or as a conclusion inferred from the character of the world or part of it. In addition, the believer's relation to God is completely different from the nonrelation metaphysics describes, so that "God" functions in a religious context as concept rather than as the name of a locatable thing, and the "knowledge" of God, if that is the right term, is likewise the use believers make of the concept in orienting their lives toward and in the light of the concept "God."

But in speaking of using religious concepts for such orientation of life, we have touched on another aspect of Phillips's description of theology. For Phillips is concerned that what he said might be taken as a plea for self-contained language games, and he doesn't want to be guilty of that. People have to see the point of religion in their lives, and this can't be done simply by distinguishing between religion and other modes of social life. Learning verbal expressions is a matter of connecting them with contexts other than those in which they are being used just then and there. The difference between a rehearsal for worship and the actual thing doesn't have to do with responses to specific signs, because those may be equally correct both times. "The difference has to do with the point the activity has in the life of the worshippers, the bearing it has on other features of their lives. Religion has something to say about aspects of human existence which are quite intelligible without reference to religion: birth, death, joy, misery, despair, hope, fortune and misfortune."[22]

The meaning of religious beliefs is thus *partly* dependent on features of human life outside religion. But the qualification "partly" indicates that this nonreligious dependence is not a relation of *justification* of these beliefs, or one of a conclusion to its grounds.[23] (Of course, one wouldn't think that that's the point for a theologian anyway, whether it is for a philosopher or not.) The theologian's question tends to be about the other part in "partly." Is there any way of telling how the concepts Phillips calls "religious beliefs" function *in addition* to their functioning in believers' lives? It's at that point that the distinctiveness of this type comes out most clearly, and not at the point of Phillips's often very powerful way of exemplifying the difference religious beliefs make in life.

We know, he tells us, that we can tell the difference between mistakes and religious beliefs. If a young mother asks the Blessed Virgin Mary to protect her newborn child, and this action is taken to be a route to a hoped-for result that could be reached by other paths, then religion is a lucky charm, a superstition; it is a mistake. If it is an act of veneration and thanksgiving, an "act of greeting" with which a number of associated beliefs and attitudes are connected, then we have religion. Religion here is rather like learning to use a picture in those cases where it is absurd to ask to be shown what the picture pictures.[24] The picture doesn't function like a hypothesis to be believed in. How *does* the picture function in addition to the way it functions as an expression of the mother's attitudes? Again, I say it's a matter of the *other* part of the meaning being *partly* dependent on crossing over to human life outside religion. So far as I can see, no other crossover or overlap has been permitted by Phillips. He is a parsimonious man, and we know what he thinks of beliefs as assertions, since he thinks assertions belong to a class with identifiable criteria for their assessment, and religion isn't like that. To cut a not very long but very repetitious story short: "But what about the protection sought for the child? What is important to recognize is that the protection must be understood in terms of these beliefs and attitudes [wonder, gratitude, humility, recognition of life as God's gift]. These virtues and attitudes are all contained in the person of Mary, the mother of Jesus. For the believer she is the paradigm of these virtues and attitudes. They constitute her holiness."[25] In other words, for the other part of "partly" we are referred back to the party of the first part, the prereligious life or nonreligious life attitudes.

I do not say that this is "reductive" of theology, that is, that it equates theological statements exhaustively with the nurturing of Christian concepts as life attitudes; even if it *were* reductive in this sense, it would be a reduction to a most significant, conceptual task. But I think that it cannot be very easy for Phillips to state (certainly not as philosopher, but not even as theologian) what a Christian believes about God and Jesus Christ, about creation and redemption, about the true nature of the Church, about divine grace and human works, about Scripture as Word of God, and so on—in other words, those beliefs that are part of the ruled language of Christian self-description, part of the language of theology, of doctrine—beliefs that must not be *separated* from *coming to* and *exercising* faith, but must be *distinguished* from these functions. The internal logic of belief is not identical with the logic of how one comes to be a Christian and live Christian concepts or, for that matter, how one unlearns them into skepticism. These things, too, may obey an internal kind of logic (or several), but it is not the same as the internal logic implicit in the interconnection of doctrines.

In the end, then, while Christian theology, for Phillips, is Christian self-description in the context of the community, responsible to it and to the God to whom the community itself is responsible, that self-description functions largely in a personal way, as indeed it should. To learn the language of the Christian community is not to undergo a profound "experience" of a privileged sort, but to learn to make that language one's own, in faith, hope, and love. But you have to take it wholesale for Phillips. To discriminate within that tradition and say, "This is a better way to express it than that; this is normative and that is peripheral," and, above all, to decide what is more than attitudinal within the communal self-description and how, what could be taken to be appropriate conceptual redescriptions of specific beliefs in our day, and how they are authorized within community and tradition— why, for guidance in that kind of task, which is the very modest but also fairly central task of that modest second-order discipline called systematic or dogmatic theology, we'd best look elsewhere than to D. Z. Phillips.

Although Phillips started out to draw the sharpest kind of distinction between Christian self-description and external description, there is a tendency in the opposite direction, in a nonspeculative way that does the same duty for him that in a very different, speculative way phenomenology does for Tracy and, in some views, for Schleiermacher.

For them, the meaning of Christian concepts is the specifically Christian way in which they shape religious consciousness. For Phillips, it is the way in which they help us dispose ourselves Christianly and affectively toward the important matters of life. But when we ask about any kind of overlap with other modes of discourse that would help us both to render and make accessible a responsible redescription of biblical and traditional beliefs, both in order to understand them and to appraise them critically in the light of that which—Him or Her who is the ultimate Ruler of Scripture, tradition, and Christian conscience— when we try to get help from Phillips on these matters we find not so much that he objects as that he has simply dematerialized. In matters of doctrinal statement, pure self-confinement to Christian self-description means no self-description. To the extent that this situation is a product of making theology purely internal to the religion, its result is a theology of total silence when one cannot simply and un-critically parrot biblical and traditional formulae. To the extent that this absence of doctrinal self-description is the result of absolutizing and rigidifying the warranted, indeed essential, distinction between religious statements and statements about religion, it is a function of the dominance of a philosophical theory or negative criteriology over theology as Christian self-description. A paradoxical result indeed.

There is no need to waste time over the application of this view to the sensus literalis, there being no *criteria* as to *what* would be appropriate redescription, or, in all likelihood, permission for the employment in the first place of any "borrowed" concepts or conceptual schemes in reading Scripture. The sensus literalis here is logically equivalent to sheer repetition of the same words. That is hardly how it has functioned in the Christian interpretive tradition.

5 /////////////////////// **Some Implications**

for Biblical Interpretation //////

How does the kind of layout we have prepared for ourselves influence one's choice or choices in regard to biblical interpretation? A lot depends on what one wishes to do. It is not the case, of course, that one of these types, even if one finds a pure representative for it, will guide us to a right interpretation of the Bible. For let us assume that the notion of a right interpretation of the Bible is itself not meaningless, but it is eschatological. The Christian community is gathered in *hope*, and that extends to as ordinary a task as that of a common way of reading its sacred text. One may take the Church through time and space to be, among other things, not a babble of voices talking completely past one another, but a groping and imperfect community of interpretation possessing a common language sufficient for people by and large who do biblical interpretation seriously, whether as technicians or simply as adherents looking for help in life and belief. And looking to the Bible and to each other for help in life and belief, these people by and large *agree* with each other enough so that they can *disagree*—for even that is an important form of agreement. The history, for example, of the exegesis of the Epistle to the Romans does not take place in a cultural or historical vacuum. It is a story of constantly varying ideologies; but it is not a story of one thing after another. There are common themes that allow one to ask how Paul sees Jesus Christ in relation to the Law; whether justification by faith is as central a motif in the Epistle as Lutherans have assumed it is; what part Paul's plea in chapters 9 and 10 in behalf of his brethren, his kinsmen according to the flesh, plays in the Epistle; and what the proper context is in which to put his imperative that every soul should be subject to the higher powers.

One tends to forget that at times it is much easier to agree on what a text says than on how to understand what the text says or how to understand how one can agree or disagree on what the text says. If a sacred text is regarded first of all, though perhaps not only, as a text that has its normative status not by virtue of mysterious inherent properties but through the functions it performs within the community for which it is a common sacred text, as Professor Kelsey has reminded us,[1] then the result is a very different kind of reading—with all the exegetical disagreements that may make the community of interpretation a cacophonous one—than would be the case if the history of exegesis were nothing more than "a map of misreading,"[2] to cite an eloquent phrase by Professor Harold Bloom, or a succession of readings that is nothing but a series of ignorant armies clashing by night, as Frank Kermode has recently proposed.[3] If that is not the case, if there *is* a community of interpretation, a tradition for which this is the sacred text, its analogue might be one school of British moralists in the eighteenth century: right exegesis, like right moral sentiment and action, is what sane, judicious, and fair-minded judges declare it to be. I do not mean to subvert hideously difficult questions about the meaning of the text and how one can get at it, but I do think that if, within a community and also without, later judges say that a certain form of combination—say, a very vivid allegorical reading; or a particular figural interpretation of the Old Testament within the New, undertaken as part of the later interpretive tradition—if this finally stretches the imagination to the breaking point, as the Antiochene theologians said about the school of Origen, then that assessment probably sets reasonable bounds to what can and cannot be done. Even then, the existence of limits does not mean that one cannot exceed them as a private scholar, but only that as an adherent who speaks for the common community of interpretation, one has probably at that point gone too far, even if that is a judgment that ought always to be made provisionally and had best be made in retrospect, except where the love of God and neighbor—those ultimate norms of Christian life and thought—are immediately at stake.

Clearly, there is no such thing as a community's assuming dictatorship of interpretation principles. Therefore, let us briefly explore how the five types that have been set forth would bear on principles of biblical reading. The only really important distinction here is that between the two basic approaches to theology: theology as one discipline in an academic class of disciplines, chiefly related to philosophy though also to philosophically grounded specific sciences' specific descriptions of Christianity, on the one hand, or theology as Christian self-description that subordinates unsystematically the philosophical and "scientific" or specific external description concerned, on the other. In the foregoing, it must be clear that I have already assumed the priority of the second kind of theology: I have no desire to be dogmatic about it, but I think that only where there is a community of interpretation and only where the interpretive enterprise considers itself accountable to the community as a whole, can the sort of agreement and disagreement that I described earlier arise. I propose to do two things: first, to ask if the five types of theological method have any bearing on principles of biblical interpretation, and, second, to examine the literal sense and how it arises in the context of this typology, as well as what some of its varieties may be—because it is by no means a unitary idea.

Type 1

Immanuel Kant's *Religion within the Limits of Reason* is a book I would pack for a long stay on a desert island. It is also a convenient example of Gordon Kaufman's *Essay on Theological Method* at work on biblical exegesis. Kant tells us that what the author intended to say is far less important than what a reasonable mind can make of what he or she wrote—the reasonable constructs the writing provides. But if the text is what Frank Kermode calls a "good enough" text, it ought to be abstractable from its setting and become instructive for reasonable minds at any point along the time-scale. That quality of being good enough in its own right so that it can be lifted out of its setting, of course, also allows the reasonable reader to take his or her place alongside the expert, the biblical scholar of technical competence. Critics have their own modest craft and integrity and let them not be ashamed of them, but let them never think either that what they do is of front-rank importance. Kant would never have agreed with D. F. Strauss, for whom theological conclusions had to be compatible with—indeed, based on—the prior results of historical-critical readings. For Kant, it is the person who has his or her rational and moral act together who is a good reader of the Bible, because it is only in terms of rational morality that the Bible can be interpreted. It is only in terms of a rational, moral understanding of our duties, freely imposed by ourselves upon ourselves—but in the Bible set forth as divine commands—that we can understand what the Bible is saying. It is only in these terms that we can select among the stories and images that are fit. Kant is traditional enough to accept the framework first provided by the apostle Paul of reading Jewish scriptures as an Old Testament incomplete in itself and leading as it were by its own thrust to its climactic fulfillment in the New. In other words, he reads the whole Bible as one story. To the Jewish reader this would be a piece of what Harold Bloom has so powerfully analyzed as a "strong misreading of the precursor."[4]

But Kant was, far more than he knew, within the Christian interpretive tradition. For him, every *persona* that he discovered in the Bible was a mark or stage along a single-storied succession, none of which took place in time; instead, each is a stage in the self-understanding and self-improvement of the moral reasoner. The biblical story as a whole, and every part of it, is an allegory. There is Adam, who is really the moral reasoner as freely disobedient to his own rational freedom. There is the incarnate Christ, who is the archetype of humanity well-pleasing to God, ineradicable in the moral reasoner's mind. Jesus is an allegorical image of this archetype, as though it were a person instead of a principle. And there is the same Christ who becomes an allegory (in individual shape) of the split between radical evil and a new disposition for good within the moral reasoner—an allegory of personal unity in the transition from one to the other. He is the allegory of reconciliation in individuated, "external" form to these two inward states. There the allegorization actually stops. For the Church is not an allegory but simply a temporal vehicle for or expression of the universal religion, the Kingdom of God that is a symbol for Kant's realm of ends. There is not only allegory here, but allegory strictly according to a moral and rational principle of interpretation, which is a universal standard and can therefore select what it will from the Scripture and leave out, of course, what is not fit. The community's sacred text becomes a partial, culturally conditioned exemplification of the universal religion. Its place as a sacred text with a certain degree of authority in the specific religious community is something to be respected as interesting, and part of the cultural map, but it is not of fundamental significance.

Type 2

For the second type, "authority" is probably also not an important concept to apply to Scripture, but "sacredness", in contrast to Kant's and Kaufman's position, is. Authority does not strike a numinous spark in the phenomenological breast because phenomenology is a reflexive examination of the self as consciousness. Schleiermacher described his version of that examination (too bad for him, but good for us, that he was brought up when the incredible complexity of phenomenological techniques had not yet developed) as "just a little introspection." But if you think that the self, simple or complex, is to be introspected, you will not come across authority very easily, because authority—as the late-eighteenth- and early-nineteenth-century rebels against Christian orthodoxy rightly discerned—usually takes the shape of something coming from without, something that smells suspiciously like the dreaded disease of heteronomy. So authority is out, for that reason as well as for the fact that authority usually functions where the community provides a context that is important for the conceptualization of its members' activities, and as we saw that is not the case for the second type. Instead, then, sacredness would be more acceptable, for it could be conceived of as one of those "meanings," or "dimensions," those "essences" present to consciousness, filled with power and resonant in the mediated, metaphorical representation of their presentational immediacy. The sacred is almost invariably represented in story form, and, happily enough, that is what we also find in the New Testament.

One finds in the New Testament that everything points us from or by means of a certain use of language to the presence of an experience that we ourselves likewise find mediated to ourselves in our time by means of language, in which description is in the employ of the self-expression of consciousness. Language becomes a mediation or expressive force at once pointing toward and projecting from that immediate consciousness which is prior to language. In other words, what one deals with is the replication of experience, and yet, because experience is never present in raw form, it is not a universal datum in the same way that concepts with their direct public accessibility are. The use of the New Testament, thus, is not rational or allegorical or purely imagistic in such a way that image is merely a paraphrase for conceptual construct, as it is for Kant and also for the methods prescribed by Professor Kaufman for theology. No, it is precisely the fact that experience has to be indirectly expressed and evoked that makes it necessary to *correlate* New Testament language and contemporary religious experience in Professor Tracy's view. Happily, the job, for all its architectonic complexity and solemnity, is not really terribly difficult. To indicate that the straightforward literal description or reference to the ordinary world is not what is at stake in the New Testament, one has to pay close attention to the literary forms, and we find that the New Testament engages us by the use of a kind of a double or split reference, as Professor Ricoeur put it, in which the *real* meaning is the innovative linguistic thrust from the first to a second level, to a newly created linguistic world, and it is this second rather than the first referent that gives us the true referent or meaning of the language. Since in its proverbs, eschatological sayings, and parables, the New Testament consistently "goes to the limits" of language through procedures like intensification and transgression, the interpreter can legitimately describe its language as a limit-language of a genuinely religious character.

Tracy finds these procedures in the proverbial sayings, the proclamatory sayings, and above all in the parables of Jesus. Especially in the case of the latter, once the strictly preliminary historical analysis has been done, we get down to the real business of showing "how the actual language form of the New Testament parables linguistically discloses the 'limit vision' of Christian eschatology . . . how that 'limit vision' in turn can be adequately articulated only in a 'limit language.' "[5] We recall of course that any decent religious experience is a preconceptual limit experience, which comes at the edge of our experiential horizon, so close to it that beyond it lies that unfathomable dimension, the transcendent. What we find out, not surprisingly, is that parables are really extended metaphors in which there is a tension between key terms, and that their tensed interaction permits their innovative projection toward a new, unforeseen referent. Again, not suprisingly, it turns out that what we have in the New Testament is really a basic form of metaphorical language which, in contrast with metaphors of normalcy, takes us to the metaphorical world of the limit, the limit in language and the limit in experience. The limit vision that we find embodied in the parables of Jesus—the wicked husbandman, the great feast, the prodigal son—is achieved precisely through their very everydayness, which heightens the eccentricity of those modes of behavior to which the Kingdom of God is compared (p. 130). Finally, that metaphorical and transgressive language disclose, which is what linguistic business is all about, a possible mode-of-being-in-the-world, that of living with explicit faith, with complete trust, with unrestricted love. The language of the New Testament disorients us and forces us to see another, seemingly impossible way of living with authenticity. As parabolic, that language redescribes our experience in such a manner that the sense of its meaning (its now limit-metaphor) discloses "a limit-referent which projects and promises that one can in fact live a life of wholeness, of total commitment, or radical honesty and agapic love in the presence of the Jesus Christ" (p. 136).

In a way, the story of the gospel by itself becomes an extended metaphor of this sort; again, what we need is a correlation, a new disclosure of a possible mode-of-being-in-the-world that will fit with our contemporary limit experience in such a way that it becomes a possible instrument of disclosure of transcendence to it. In this sense, and without prejudice to its historicity in the ordinary sense, Tracy can call the gospel story the Christian's "supreme fiction" (p. 204). For that is its functioned place: like any powerful story, it has the force of disclosing our present limit situation and opening up a new possibility. It turns out that the Christian symbols—so Professor Tracy finds not by any compelling argument but simply by way of testimony to experience—still have, despite doubts about their efficacy, the power to shape contemporary religious experience. That is especially true of the Christian "fact," the story—I called it an extended parable— of Jesus in the Gospels, which includes his words and deeds, his destiny, the expression of messiahship, and so on. They all re-present the possibility of the agapic mode-of-being-in-the-world as an existential possibility now. And by "fact" Tracy means not the "scandal of particularity," of salvation here and now being dependent on one person then and there. The "fact" is the re-presentation, the preserving of a certain possibility by uneasy disclosive symbolic language and action. For Tracy as for Rudolf Bultmann, the Christian "fact" is the proclamation through word and sacrament of the singular history of Jesus as the Christ. "Fact" or "event" is expressive language given-and-received.

Tracy's language is tortuous and complex, but his intention is clear. What the story of Jesus is about is not Jesus storied or historical, but "existential possibility," which is not a temporal cumulative qualification of a specific character in his or her own story, but a successful or unsuccessful evocation of a mode of present consciousness. For Kant (and Gordon Kaufman), Jesus Christ was an allegory or image of an archetype of universal reason. For Professor Tracy, the fruit of New Testament interpretation is that Jesus Christ is a most powerful symbol; his reality, an idealization of the represencing, through the expressive and evocative language of the story, of his life-stance. That is what such stories do: by expressing such stances they presence them for and in our own life-stances. To put not too fine a point on it (but, I hope, not unfairly all the same), sacredness in the form of a limit-mode-of-being-in-the-world has had its due. The experience of limit and of the "condition of its possibility," the transcendent ("God"), could not have been more vigorously affirmed. But something else may have emerged with clarity. Allegory there, symbol here—the first two types of theological procedure, when observed at the level of biblical interpretation, have little use for any form of the literal sense. Archaic or anachronistic it would be termed, threatening with the notorious *sacrificium intellectus* any person who, having finally got past the historical critic's claim to regulatory agency power over what may pass for abiding religious meaning in the New Testament, was beginning to ask about the literal sense. For both the first and second types, it is obvious that there is no intrinsic need to have the moral reasoner focus on Jesus Christ for his or her self-understanding, or for the symbolizing consciousness to be expressed by this particular "fiction" to actualize its agapic possibility now.

Again, for both allegorical-rational interpretation and for symbolic-experiential interpretation, the apparent literal sense of the New Testament, in which Jesus as "real" or "historical" seems to have an irreducibly unique and unsurpassable place in relation to salvation, is quite dispensable. Kant is clear on this matter. He said that the rational archetype obviously cannot be turned into a single individual who would fully embody it, and thereby set the stage for a long argument. He said that doing so would be confusing story with reason, and would turn the story into a childish superstition. David Tracy turns quite stern at this point and follows Schubert Ogden in denying that the New Testament really prescribes what he calls the "fundamentalist and Barthian" "exclusivist Christocentrism." Symbolic-experiential Christology thinks of Jesus or rather the story of Jesus (why not both?) as perhaps the highest re-presentation of the authentic agapic mode, but certainly not unique or indispensable. "What that special occasion . . . manifests is the disclosure that the only God present to all humanity at every time and place . . . is present explicitly, actually, decisively, as my God in my response to this Jesus as the Christ" (pp. 206ff.). No doubt the decisiveness would remain if the story of a response to it remained—in distinction from the historical Jesus who need not have been, and need not have been as he is portrayed. So the literal sense is left far behind in both allegorical and symbolic interpretation. This is really not surprising from any number of points of view, particularly since neither of these types, in assigning priority to theology as an academic discipline, owes any allegiance—it has no obligation to do so—to Christian self-description as normed by the religious community with its traditional linguistic forms. Categorically, Tracy, certainly, and Kaufman, implicitly, are still governed by the sharp distinction— and conjunction—of meaning as "sense" and meaning as "reference." Tracy, in particular, like his master in this respect, Schubert Ogden, seeks to affirm not only that the *storied* sense and reference is not the storied sense but present existence, but that the *historical* referent, in harmony with this view, can only be Jesus as *one* historical instance embodying life in accordance with God's wishes, even if relatively the best one. The two outlooks, on the meaning of the story and on the historical Jesus, are quite compatible with each other. What is interesting is the extent to which the whole complex "sense and reference" implicit here is still ruled by a relation between Jesus' story and his history that is typical of a nineteenth-century view of the "literal" sense and by a single as well as doubtful philosophical theory about "meaning." But in one parenthetical sense, one may express a certain relief over moving from Kaufman to Tracy. Tracy, like Paul Tillich, tells us that symbols may well die, and of course the Christ symbol may be among those dead ones, even though Tracy believes it isn't so—at least not yet. Both the life arena and the graveyard of religious symbols is the history of culture understood as the history of collective or cultural consciousness.

Now one needs to say that to the extent that the name and title Jesus Christ function within the sociolinguistic context of the specific community called Christian, and theological talk about "Jesus Christ" is part of the self-description of Christianity, the language rules are such that culture as the history of collective consciousness and its linguistic self-expressions are simply not apt representations of how the process works. We are in a different language game. The name and title Jesus Christ neither "come to life" nor "die" in the Christian community. It's a different language game with a different grammar. Still, it is a relief to have symbols that live and die organically rather than having images paraphrasing rational constructs that are brought about by deliberate analytical (as for Kaufman) reflections, so that, say, the image of God as monarch may be abolished by scholarly theological committee vote under the auspices of the A.A.R., and a prize issued for the invention of a more fitting image for these times, which are, on the one hand, threatened by complete self-destruction in nuclear war and, on the other hand, obviously no longer mythical or absolutist in political sentiment. The "Suffering Servant" image for God and for Christ is always all right as long as it is not taken to provide religious legitimacy for the status of non-unionized domestic help. But enough.

Type 3

When we then turn to type 3, the situation gets more complex because we are now in territory where there is a far clearer endeavor to correlate theology as academic discipline and as Christian self-description. It is well to recall that in *The Christian Faith* Schleiermacher treats of "Holy Scripture" under his doctrine of the Church, and there, more specifically, under his enumeration of the permanent features of the Church in its subsistence alongside the world. Freely translating, we may say that he puts Scripture in about the same place where a social scientist, analyzing the Church as a typical religious community, would put it. There are rituals like baptism and communion, as well as other authorized functions, a professional class, and a sacred text in the community. It is not surprising that Schleiermacher says that one must "avoid the impression that a doctrine must belong to Christianity because it is contained in Scripture, whereas in point of fact it is only contained in Scripture because it belongs to Christianity."[6]

The New Testament is simply an authoritative or normative expression of the pious Christian self-consciousness of the first Christians, and indirectly the self-communication of the perfect God-consciousness of Jesus Christ through *that* derived communal God-consciousness before, within, and after Scripture. One notes immediately Schleiermacher's correlationist views at work. The understanding of the "essence" of Christianity is indeed determined by that academic criterion: the sense of absolute dependence as the universal form underlying every positive religion and making all positive religions individually and on a common scale susceptible to systematic analysis. At the same time, this study—given the co-inherence of positive religion (i.e., Christianity) with the feeling of absolute dependence (i.e., religion)—is part of the self-description of the Christian Church and has the practical purpose of "governance" (i.e., practical membership in the community) as its goal. Scripture is part of that larger institutionalized complex which is the Christian community, to which all Christian self-description must be accountable. Schleiermacher thus faces the necessity of restating in contemporary (and Protestant!), rather than past cultural, linguistic coinage, the same experience of the same community that has been articulated ever since the beginning of Christianity. In other words, unlike Tracy, Schleiermacher knows no higher correlation in scriptural exegesis than the correlation of normed Christian language, on the one hand, and Christian religious experience on the other hand. Unlike Tracy, Schleiermacher could not subsume the two sides of this correlation under a higher synthesis, such as a theory of re-presentation of a possible mode-of-being-in-the-world for present actualization, and think that he had exhausted the sense of the text, especially a Christological text, through such a refined mergence of the temporal or chronological dimension of past and present within consciousness.

For Schleiermacher, then, the history of communal consciousness that he was engaged in was neither simply a historical-cultural process nor the existential merging of a symbol from the past in present, contemporaneous consciousness. Instead, that history was, among other things, the history of an interpretive tradition under the categoreal scheme of communal consciousness or self-consciousness. And an irreducible, even privileged part of that tradition was the referring of Scripture and its reading to that Christian context. This is one way of discussing the literal sense. One meaning of "literal reading of Scripture" is the Church's understanding of Scripture *if* one can show a genuine continuity in that respect. Schleiermacher thought he could. With regard to the christological texts, he thought the consensus of the Church is that they refer literally to Jesus as the originator of our experience or self-understanding as redeemed sinners within the Church. He thought the proper way to show such continuity was by co-reference to consciousness rather than to Christ by means of ideas.

But the co-reference did not submerge Christ or draw Christ into itself, as is the case for someone like Tracy. The Christ event is not a symbol for present self-understanding; it is, rather, the life of Jesus of Nazareth.

There was an emerging consensus in Schleiermacher's day—that is, after Kant—of which Schleiermacher was fully part. It was, in fact, a most respectable, avant-garde, high-culture academic consensus about the respectability of Christianity, when theology was joined to the more respectable discipline of philosophy, although that is certainly not how Schleiermacher himself saw the matter. The consensus held that the joint idea of incarnation and redemption was the essence of Christianity, and Christianity had to have an essence so that historical science and—more importantly in that day—philosophy could interpret it and make it respectable. Where Schleiermacher differed very clearly from Friedrich Schelling (in his early days), and perhaps a little less clearly from the much more ambiguous Hegel, was over the fact that he saw this essence not as a permanent ideal or a gradual development in the history of humankind, but as unequivocally realized in the historical individual Jesus Christ, and saw the Church as being in dependence on him. The story of the divine archetype's incarnation was the story of Jesus in the New Testament. *That* was the referent of the story, and so on that particular point Schleiermacher read the New Testament literally—and for him, of course, that meant historically. I said that the literal sense is a complex matter. It is not always under all circumstances identical with reference to a "historical" event or person, or even with a procedure to which the notion "reference" applies. But under the circumstances under which Schleiermacher read it, it was bound to be the case. He once declared passionately that he wished to have his whole theology guided by the one text that was most important to him, John 1:14: "And the Word was made flesh and dwelt among us and we beheld his glory, the glory as of the only begotten of the Father, full of grace and truth." That Word incarnate was the Redeemer experienced in Christian consciousness and church, *and* the person described in the Gospels taken as a source of historical information.

Let us recall that correlation to Schleiermacher meant at one and the same time the autonomy of two independent factors as well as their direct reciprocity, not their common coherence under an explanatory system, as Hegel had it. In regard to biblical interpretation, especially

Christological interpretation, this correlation meant to Schleiermacher that he thought he should and could show that a modern, purely historical interpretation of the story of the historical Jesus depicted in the New Testament and an equally modern theological reading of Jesus as the unique, fully incarnate archetypal and unsurpassable originator of Christian God-consciousness would be compatible with each other, arriving at the same result: the absolute uniqueness and unsurpassable finality of Jesus' full and undisturbed God-consciousness. Debate about the success of this venture was intense and harsh, David Friedrich Strauss in all probability delivering the most astute and devastating criticism, because he and F. C. Baur understood clearly that this picture depended most fully on the historical veracity of the portrait of the Gospel of John—the very gospel they took to be not only the latest but the least historical and most theological. Strauss, like Ernst Troeltsch and Van Harvey after him, argued that what Schleiermacher had actually demonstrated was the very contrary of his own intention. He had shown the impossibility of thinking of any person as being at one and the same time fully ingredient in the natural chain of causal history and qualitatively, absolutely unique. Despite himself, Schleiermacher had demonstrated that in order to argue such a claim from the Gospels, historical exegesis must be forced by theological intent and by a slippery anthropology that avoids—unsuccessfully, at that—the supernatural constitution of Christ in the depiction of him in the Gospels. Schleiermacher's attempt was, Strauss and Baur agreed, a special instance of the Christological dogma's dilemma: how to show forth both the presence of two unabridged natures and their full union in one completely unitary person. The critics proposed that the dilemma in present-day, specifically modern form was not metaphysical but that of trying to think of unique divine revelation in history.

But for our purposes, Schleiermacher's success, or lack of it, is peripheral. The main point is that the balance between the two types of theology in this correlation, academic and church-oriented, leads to a serious consideration of the literal sense at at least one crucial point within the New Testament, that is, the story of Jesus. One is tempted to ask if there are other representatives of this same correlationist type, and I would propose that serious consideration of Paul Tillich—as Schleiermacher redivivus in this respect, while not a foregone conclusion—might be eminently worthwhile. It is possible that some of the so-called right-wing followers of Rudolf Bultmann—Ernst Fuchs, Gerhard Ebeling, Ernst Käsemann, and James Robinson in his "new quest" for the historical Jesus—also belong to his guild. Never mind the proliferation of names; the important point to bear in mind is that even though David Tracy calls his a theology of correlation, a person like Schleiermacher has, from the specific vantage point of this study, a far greater right to do so, for the correlation both in fundamental method and in principles of biblical exegesis is not subsumed under a common, foundational philosophical structure. And not being so subsumed, the sensus literalis arises as a natural mode of biblical reading.

Type 3: Mediating Theology Without System

Schleiermacher is a controversial case because many writers have consigned him to the second type; Professor Brian Gerrish of Chicago tends in that direction. But Professor Stephen Sykes tends to agree with me. The point here is that Schleiermacher identifies theology in two ways: as a practical discipline whose unity lies in its aim, the training of people in the conceptual skills necessary for ministry in the community defined by specific Christian life and language use; and as a historical and philosophical inquiry into the "essence" of Christianity, that is, as an academic discipline grounded in a unitary theory of explanation for all disciplines and in human nature. As a matter of fact, it was this polarity in Schleiermacher that inspired my typology in the first place. On the one hand, Schleiermacher, in his *Brief Outline of the Study of Theology*, gives clear priority to the practical aim over the scientific character of theology and says very specifically that, like law and medicine, theology as a "positive science" cannot be grounded in a general theory of explanation. On the other hand, there is no more drastic or consistent case of the "turn to the subject" than Schleiermacher's own dogmatic theology, *The Christian Faith*. In paragraph 30 he says that all statements in dogmatic theology take three forms (a famous or notorious remark): they are statements about God, they are descriptions of the world, and they are expressions of the condition of the self.[1] Later he adds not only that the last of these three forms is the basic one, but that in the best of theological worlds it would be the *only* form in which theological statements are cast. It is really the turn to the subject with a vengeance. Earlier on he had stated that all *religious* statements are reports about the immediate consciousness of ourselves as absolutely dependent, "which is the same thing, of being

70

in relation to God."[2] His immediate consciousness is a bit like David Tracy's and Bernard Lonergan's unqualified love (that is, love unlimited by any finite object) or like Paul Tillich's notion of faith as absolute concern which meets its true object precisely by having no finite object but being in the unqualified mode. Notice that Schleiermacher does *not* say: From the feeling of absolute dependence I make the inferential move to the presence of God—no, the feeling itself is the relation; God is co-present in *that* specific modification of my presence to myself.

But then Schleiermacher drops a very interesting remark. He has asked what one could mean by immediate self-consciousness in contrast to the other two basic capacities through which the human subject realizes himself: knowing and willing. This is not an easy question to answer: you never have a pure instance of immediate self-consciousness, as you may have with knowing and willing, and, further, self-consciousness is experientially prior to language and thus prior to any interpretation we put on it. He says that the best we can say is that it simply consists of "affective receptivity" or "the feeling of dependence" and "spontaneous activity" or "the feeling of freedom." And then he drops the remark, "To these propositions assent can be unconditionally demanded." How so, we ask? "No one will deny them who is capable of a little introspection and can find interest in the real subject of our present inquiries."[3]

The systematic principle, that of immediate self-consciousness or "feeling," is the principle of correlation between the distinctively religious mode (including the Christian mode faith, as Schleiermacher calls it) and the general character of human being and human meaning. What is fascinating here is the low level of intellectual force he considers it to require. "A little introspection," rather like common sense—nothing high-powered here! It's as though the principle of correlation *could* have been something else if he hadn't lived in Prussia when he did and experienced the philosophical possibilities of his time. General criteria for meaning on the one side, the specificity of Christian faith and language on the other, and an ad hoc conceptual instrument for bringing them together—distinctiveness and reciprocity together. (But certainly no confusion between Christian doctrine and philosophical ideas about God!)

In sum, general criteria of meaning are not nearly as foundational in type 3 as they are in type 2. But the real litmus test of this correlation between the two approaches comes in the application, and in Schleiermacher's case Christology is the crucial case. It was, you recall, David Friedrich Strauss who coined these sobering words: "Schleiermacher's *The Christian Faith* has really but a single dogma, that concerning the person of Christ. . . . Schleiermacher's Christology is a last attempt to make the churchly Christ acceptable to the modern world. . . . The illusion which is supported primarily by Schleiermacher's explanations, that Jesus could have been a man in the full sense and still as a single person stand above the whole of humanity, is the chain which still blocks the harbor of Christian theology against the sea of rational science."[4] These words were written thirty years after Schleiermacher's death, on the occasion of the posthumous publication of Schleiermacher's lectures on the life of Jesus. They were in no way a triumph. Schleiermacher could not follow Hegel in the claim that history was an aspect of reason. While he believed in the kind of nonscientific history, the transmission of a tradition, that to him was virtually identical with the divine spirit, he saw history far more as an empirical study than Hegel had done; Hegel despised the scientific study of history. Schleiermacher was fully modern in not believing that one could *deduce* a specific historical fact such as Jesus. Instead, one had to account for it after the event by the rules of evidence. Schleiermacher acknowledged that the Jesus of history (a term he did not use) and the Christ of faith (likewise) belonged together and were one, and he wanted to show that they were. To the best of my knowledge, it was D. F. Strauss who first used them, but it was in analyzing and arguing against Schleiermacher that he first did so. Schleiermacher was not at all successful in his attempt. There is absolutely no doubt that for him, unlike David Tracy, the ascriptive subject of the New Testament texts (clearly and unambiguously) was Jesus—and Jesus, Schleiermacher further wished to affirm, in his uniqueness and finality for Christian faith. In fact, Schleiermacher set his face quite deliberately against the rationalist allegorical reading of Christianity, in which Jesus was a teacher and an example, and no more.

Schleiermacher's thought was subtle, complex, and highly nuanced—and God knows he needed these qualities; he had to adjust a great many simultaneous and all too competitive interests. One of the most pressing was to argue the case that the believer has access to the Savior or Redeemer (the designations Schleiermacher usually preferred to the name "Jesus") in a way different from that of the historian.

Once Schleiermacher got past the introduction to *The Christian Faith*, his main point was to suggest that the whole of systematic or dogmatic theology was to be understood and organized "by the facts of the religious self-consciousness" as they are determined by the antithesis of sin and grace;[5] Schleiermacher had a "subjective correlative" (if I may invert T. S. Eliot's famous term) for every objective or specifically Christian concept, whether the correlation was drawn tightly or loosely. If the former, the Christian concept was virtually irreducibly transposable into the experiental correlate; if the latter (as I have suggested), the experiential correlate was simply a kind of evocative analogue to the Christian concept. The correlate for the antithesis between sin and grace was the antithesis of the predominance of either pain or pleasure in the feeling of absolute dependence.

The meaningfulness of the notions "Redemption" and a "Redeemer" depend on this contrast as universally intelligible because universally experienceable. Some qualification is necessary here. Just as for Kierkegaard a generation later, "despair" was not identical with sin but a necessary correlate and logical precondition to it, so for Schleiermacher the antithesis of sin and grace is not identical with that of pain and pleasure but a precondition for understanding it. There is a theological reason for stressing that complex logical relation. If "sin" is part of Christian vocabulary, part of a Christian semiotic structure, it is obviously related to the concept "Christ" or "Redeemer." In fact, the case is sometimes made—Karl Barth makes it—that "sin" as concept, whatever its status as experience in our lives, is logically dependent on "Christ" as the prior concept; that the logic of belief is quite different from, not necessarily contrary to but independent of, the logic or movement of coming to believe. We don't know—so the theological logic would go in that case—that we are sinners except that we have been redeemed ("I was converted on Calvary," as Friedrich Kohlbrugge said). Schleiermacher wanted it both ways: "Sin" and "Redeemer" presuppose each other; they are *mutually implicated* dogmatic concepts, and more than that you don't have to say (can't say?) as long as you grant some experiential correlation to the logical coupling in which there is a relative priority of not sin but some experiential equivalent over the experiential equivalent of grace. In that cautious and complex manner, and with the turn to the subject—that is, to self-consciousness as the criterion for general meaningfulness—Schleiermacher joined John Locke in suggesting that the meaningfulness of something general or universal is the logical and real precondition for the meaningfulness of the particular, the concept of a "Redeemer."

Does this all sound abstract and logic-chopping? Far removed from real religious experience? But consider the following, at least as a possibility, certainly no more, not as a rigid, dogmatic statement: the language we use is what enables us to experience in the first place. There is no such thing as a non-interpreted, nonlinguistic experience: language is a social, not an individual structure or system. Our *Christian* experience is not a solo flight but our experience within the linguistic network, the changing and yet recognizably continuous language structure, the worshiping and moral pattern of the Christian community. Theology is therefore not simply a redescription of the expressions of a first-level conceptual level faith (as Schleiermacher thought) but also a second-level redescription of the contemporary forms, related to the past tradition, of the language of the Christian Church, as Schleiermacher also thought. It is the endeavor to articulate the grammar or internal logic of that language under its own norm or norms.

And now to return to that "internal logic" for Schleiermacher: the antithesis of sin and grace. For him, as for type 3 in general, the transition from the one to the other is made *possible* by the redemption wrought by Jesus of Nazareth. So Schleiermacher has to describe both what takes place in the *actual* turn that we ourselves must undertake—which falls beyond the scope of the present project—and also how the possibility can be accounted for by the character of the Redeemer. In other words, for Schleiermacher, the subject matter of the New Testament—indeed, the very essence of Christianity—is Jesus Christ—although, it must be remembered, always Jesus Christ in relation to the Christian religious affections or the feeling of absolute dependence, not Jesus Christ without reference to faith or subjectivity: not *Christus extra nos*, but *Christus pro nobis* and *Christus in nobis*. Strauss was right that Schleiermacher's whole system was focused around the dogma Christology.

Let me very quickly touch on the doctrines of Christ's work and Christ's person, reminding you that in each case the source for what Christians say is for Schleiermacher the communal experience of the Christian tradition which has to be substantiated by but does not originate in the New Testament texts. The texts have a preeminent status only to the extent that they are the earliest and therefore presumably most authoritative descriptions of communal Christian experience. "In this corporate life," says Schleiermacher, "which goes back to the influence of Jesus, redemption is effected by him through the communication of his sinless perfection."[6] In capsule form, what is being offered the possibility of change is our self-consciousness, which is not surprising since that is the very essence of human being. No substitutionary view! We experience this change, but neither individually nor collectively are we sufficient to effect it by ourselves. In other words, perfection as a predicate attaches neither to us nor to the Church. The change in us can only be accounted for by one who actually *is* sinless perfection—that is, steadily unclouded God-consciousness throughout his life—as we might say, tempted but never turned by temptation. Such a one would do more than merely be the historical *occasion* for the turn from sin to grace taking place in others; he would be the indispensable condition, possibility, or source of their turning. But why say *"would* be"? The theoretical condition set by individual and collective experience has been met. That there had to be an individual Redeemer in order to account for the change in others is clear. But that it was *Jesus of Nazareth* can only be demonstrated from the testimony of the record—as historical record and as description of earliest Christian experience. It is at this point, then, that the Christ of faith, the source of experience, meets the Jesus of history, the record's description of the actual person. Schleiermacher, you can see, *had* to lecture on the historical Jesus, and he did give a lecture course on the life of Jesus, which, when published, was by common consent seen to be an absolute disaster.

In the cause and effect chain by which our consciousness of redemption goes back to the Redeemer, the outward aspects and events of his life do not matter; all that matters is the perfection of his God-consciousness, externally mirrored but not constituted by what he does and undergoes—even what he *says* is only a conditioned, secondary outward expression of it. You can see that even if it were to be demonstrated that Jesus was not crucified, it wouldn't matter to Schleiermacher's outlook, for the crucial thing about his death was only the attitude manifested in it, significantly indeed but not indispensably. And he specifically says that Christian faith has no stake in the resurrection. What that faith *does* have a stake in is the incarnation, that the archetype or ideal—not of moral reason, as for Kant, but of universal God-consciousness—was fully present in him, identical with him. Like Kant, Schleiermacher took incarnation to be the identity of predicate or archetype and subject or individual, except that he as a theologian, unlike Kant, confirmed it. And unlike Tracy, Schleiermacher clearly opted for the ascriptive subject's governance of the predicate, that is, for the priority of ascriptive literalism in regard to the unitary person Jesus. Unlike Tracy, Schleiermacher does not merge or mix up two referents as meaning in the gospel stories. Jesus owns his predicates. The relation with the faith or religious self-consciousness of the recipient is the bond that Tracy sees (in *Blessed Rage*) directly in the predicate that makes Jesus one of us. Jesus is no mere example or prototype; he is, as we said, the indispensable ground or archetype of what he achieves for us. "The Redeemer, then, is like all men in virtue of the identity of human nature, but distinguished from them all by the constant potency of his God-consciousness, which was a veritable existence of God in Him."[7] This is his nature, his person; and by virtue of his *self-communication* of this being, his self-consciousness, to us, making possible the change in us, it is also his work.

Once again, we say these things not from the text so much as from the unity and continuity of Christian experience from earliest days on. All these statements about Jesus are not conceptual redescriptions of the textual portrait but redescriptions of the utterances of faith in him, descriptions of him as given in, with, and under the relation of faith, which therefore enters into what we can say about him—just as for Kant we can know the data of our intuition not in themselves but only under the organizing impact of the reason that understands them. For Schleiermacher, there is no knowledge of *Christus extra nos*, in himself; we know him only as he is related to our faith, *pro* and *in nobis*. This is the claim that there is a distinctive faith method that enables us to know the actual, historical person in a distinctive religious way and by way of a distinctive religious route. For no individual item or event in Christ's life, for no specific characteristic do you need demonstration—even if it were available. Historical method and faith method are clearly distinct. And yet! There is need to *correlate* these two distinct and autonomous procedures. Why? Once again, Schleiermacher did not proceed from a redescription of the New Testament portrait but from a connection between experience and a claimed fact responsible for it: his primary world—we might say, his world of discourse—was the general world in which "experience" and "fact" come together. He claimed that Christian experience was factually caused by a historical individual, and therefore he had a crucial stake at least in the factual existence of Jesus. Furthermore, while he knew that you cannot *demonstrate* the absolute sinlessness of an individual and probably not even *portray* it, you had best try to show at least two things: that the portraits give intimations of it, and that they do not contain incredible fact claims (healing miracles are OK; nature miracles are a problem), for if they do, the very fact of his existence might be a problem, and Schleiermacher needed that for his faith-affirmations. Schleiermacher would have agreed with those after him who said that if you claim that faith has a basis in historical fact, you cannot at the same time disallow the testing of its truth by historical method. You may keep the two procedures absolutely distinct but you must correlate them. But then you will have a very hard time staying with the priority of the subject under a literal, ascriptive reading. The historical method will reconstruct a natural person under conditions of general historical possibility, not a man who can be an exception to the very conditions under which alone historical explanation can be done—no interruption of the natural, causal scheme, uniformity of human experience, probability status and revisability of historical assertions. The very person under this kind of explanatory description is bound to be different from the person who, under the faith method or descriptions, is the perfect Redeemer.

D. F. Strauss put the general problem of Schleiermacher's *Life of Jesus*, quite apart from specific test cases, like this: "Statements that this or that 'is not harmonizable with our presuppositions about Christ,' or that 'he could be what he is in our faith only if . . . ' and so on . . . are repeated endlessly as reasons why this or that passage [in the Gospels] is to be interpreted in a certain way, or why this relation or this action of Jesus is to be understood in this way."[8]

The third type—correlation of academic discipline grounded in explanatory theory with communal Christian self-description, but with an ad hoc strategy for correlation—usually articulates the literal, ascriptive sense by correlating a description of the Jesus of history with one of the Christ of faith, remaining hermeneutically consistent (the same ascriptive subject is striven for!) but risking contradiction or sheer confusion in the endeavor to integrate theological description with historical method. Is the problem fatal, or can we say, We can cut our losses, because this correlation does not rest on a tight method but always remains an experiment and an imperfect one?

Type 4

As a theological discipline dogmatics is the scientific test to which the Christian church puts herself regarding the language about God which is peculiar to her.[9]

You will recall how I described the extreme at the *opposite* end from theology under the rubric of explanatory theory. That description seems to be encapsulated in—perhaps I really should say, pinched from—the section heading from Karl Barth's *Church Dogmatics* which I just quoted. (1) Theology involves a critical task, "a scientific" or *wissenschaftlich* test. (2) What is done theologically is done within a religious *community*, the Church; it is the communal self-description of the community, rather than the individual creed of an individual person, even if he or she is Christian. (3) Theology constitutes an inquiry into the specific language peculiar to, in fact constitutive of, the specific semiotic community called the Christian Church or churches. Incidentally, Barth wrote this passage in 1931 when most theologians still thought that the tools for knowing God were faith with or without concepts, in either case an "inward," mental instrument and not an "outward" or linguistic skill. Even philosophers were only just beginning to talk about concepts as linguistic skills, about thinking as *doing* something and doing it verbally, that is, as performative utterance. *Now* it's a commonplace, philosophically as well as theologically. But it was quite remarkable for Barth intuitively to reach that far ahead. (4) Here I admit to doing a bit of finagling or making Barth say what I want him to say—the word for that is "interpretation"—the subject matter of theology (the very word itself involves it) is "God"; that is the "object" or "referent" of the language. When I say I am interpreting Barth, what I mean is that for Barth we have the reality only under the description, only linguistically, not independently of the concept as we use it in preaching and liturgy, in action in church and world, in prayer and praise. Barth doesn't always, but logically he *should*, make a distinction not between words and concepts but between "signifier" and "signified" (to use the terms that deconstructionists employ), between the sense of the words and their *semiotic referent*, and then he should say, "Don't get these distinctions, especially the last one between semiotic sense and semiotic referent, confused with the distinction between meaning (semiotic sense and referent) and truth or reality referent." Specifically, we don't have more than our concepts of God; we don't have a separate intuition, a preconceptual or prelinguistic apprehension or grasp of God in his reality, not unless we are mystics (and we honor them). But we don't need it either; for the reality of God is given in, with, and under the concept and not separably, and that is adequate for us.

That's why Barth wrote a book interpreting St. Anselm of Canterbury's so-called ontological argument for the existence of God. For as Barth saw it, Anselm was saying that the right conceptual description of God—that than which no greater can be conceived—logically implies God's reality: for if that than which no greater can be conceived does not exist, then a greater *can* be conceived, which contradicts the description. But (1) this case in which we grasp the reality by means of a logical sequence or description is a unique case, because God and his relation to us is absolutely unique; it cannot be recapitulated in any finite instance or case of knowledge of finite reality. (2) This train of thought and its result, that God is present as the object of the intellect only in the concept or the use of the word *God*, is the meaning of the concept "faith" or "Christian faith" when used in the context of reflection on the *grammar* of the word *God* as it is used in the Christian Church. Barth does not have a single definition for the term *faith*; it is various things in various Christian contexts—the only thing they have in common is that "faith" is defined by the adjective "Christian" rather than vice versa. So you see, when Barth says "language about God peculiar to her," that is, the Church, he is still saying something descriptive about Christian language and not about matching a philosophical metaphysics with an ecclesiastical one.

So he *does* seem to be really at one extreme of the polar ends of my typology. But we ought to reserve judgment. In the next few pages after this quotation, Barth puzzles over the other extreme, theology understood as an academic discipline subject to the general criteria of a Wissenschaftstheorie, a theory of explanation—or, as it used to be called, "transcendental philosophy." He confronts it at its toughest, that is, its most formal: without basing it on a philosophy of reason based on some theory of a unitary human nature. He suggests that given the common academic use of the word *Wissenschaft*, theology doesn't qualify very well under that heading. What it has in common with other disciplines is that it is self-consistent and that, like others, "it is a human effort after a definite object of knowledge".[10] (Such an understanding of *Wissenschaft* in terms of its object came to be dismissed, and rightly so, because no self-respecting academic discipline has its method strictly specified by the object or data; at best it is an understanding of the data *under* a method or theory. The theory, not the object, has priority when you ask what kind of explanations make a given discipline a coherent field of study. What Barth might have said instead of "object of knowledge" is "conceptual referent within a specific conceptual or cultural-linguistic structure.")

He then asks, What is generally meant by science, and how is theology related to it? From an essay by his philosophical friend Heinrich Scholz he takes these statements about what constitutes explanatory theory in all fields: (1) the postulate of noncontradiction among and within propositions; (2) internal coherence; (3) testability (revisability of propositions—nondogma); (4) arrangement of all propositions into axioms and theorems, and being susceptible of demonstration on that basis. Then Barth says, that's unacceptable to theology. *Even* "the very minimum postulate of freedom from contradiction is acceptable by theology only upon the very limited interpretation, by the scientific theorist upon the scarcely tolerable one, that theology will not assert an irremovability in principle of the 'contradictions' which it is bound to make good."[11]

Now Barth means "only limited interpretation" quite literally and seriously: take the concept "incarnation." There have been many people (D. M. Baillie, for example, in *God Was in Christ*) who have said, there is a difference between contradiction and paradox. Contradiction is a logical impossibility or inconceivability, like one thing being at once itself and not itself. Paradox is a state of affairs in the real world rather than in logic, in which, for example, as for Marxists in regard to late capitalism, a social and economic situation contains self-contradictions that will cause its collapse, or, as Søren Kierkegaard, "reason is a passion which wills its own downfall." Paradox is a well-known general meaning complex, and incarnation belongs to that class. Barth responds in effect: (1) The Incarnation of God in Christ does not belong to a general "meaning" class, including "paradox"; (2) it is not a logical contradiction—*How* it is possible for a person to be at once human and divine is not intrinsically irrational, but the *condition* of its possibility, or rationality, is one we cannot know in this present finite state. With regard to the mysteries of our faith, our reasoning is not absent but fragmentary. Even the meaningfulness, to say nothing of the truth of Christian statements, is a matter of faith seeking understanding rather than faith arising from the statement of general meaning. Until we do know what can now only be the content of faith, its internal logic has the shape of a limiting rule rather than a testable proposition.

Theology, then, is by and large an exploration of the meaning of first-level Christian assertions. It is an exploration not usually of their truth, but of their meaning; it is their *re-description* in technical concepts rather than their *explanation*. It is conceptual analysis.

But if that is what Barth thinks he is doing, he does not fully or really belong to type 5; for he is not explaining but interpreting, and to that extent he has recourse, and gladly so, to philosophy, for Christianity as a semiotic system does not bring its own technical conceptual tools with it. As Schleiermacher said, it has to borrow them from elsewhere, from philosophy. Take, for example, the interpretation of the biblical text, which plays for Barth the same role as Christian experience did for Schleiermacher, so that Barth tends much more toward a sort of *literary* or conceptual-analytical reading of the biblical text rather than either a *historical* or religious- experiential one. We cannot read the text without a moment of interpretive reflection in that reading, and that means in effect that we cannot read without the use of philosophy.[12] But obviously this use of philosophy must be a ruled use.[13]

For type 4, exemplified by Barth, then, Christian self-description and general theory combine unsystematically, as for type 3. But unlike type 3, the combination here is not a correlation between equals but an unsystematic, always *ad hoc performance* of subordinating explanatory theory and philosophy more generally, as a tool in Christian communal self-description, so that in effect a conceptual scheme that may function *explanatorily* in a general or philosophical context functions only interpretively or descriptively in a Christian context. But this use, this combination, remains the constantly renewed task of Christian theology. And unlike type 5, for which there can be no "external" descriptive categories in Christian self-description, Barth very much affirms their ruled use in theology.

For the third type, like the second, there is a constant need to correlate human knowledge or experience under criteria of general meaningfulness or under a general theory of explanation with the specific self-descriptive language of the Christian community. To sharpen that statement and focus it on the figure of Jesus Christ as it is treated in each of the types, in type 3 as well as type 2 there is a need to correlate the specific ascriptive subject, Jesus, or "the Redeemer," with general criteria for the meaningfulness of the notion of redemption. In type 2, under the relentless pressure of the demand of general criteria to provide a *systematic* correlation, you do one of two things: *either* you provide an allegorical interpretation of the New Testament, in which the predicate exemplified by Jesus overpowers the ascriptive subject himself and then you return to Kant, as does David Tracy in *Blessed Rage for Order, or* your interpretation ends up having two meanings or referents at the same time, Jesus and some general experience, as Tracy does in a later book, *The Analogical Imagination.* There was nothing wrong with having two such meanings in an earlier tradition of interpretation, when you didn't have to make their coherence a matter of systematic relation under a theory of explanation, when you arranged them instead under an informal rule of priority orderings. But given the demand for systematic correlation of the two meanings, what we get instead is hermeneutical incoherence, at least in this exemplar of type 2. Furthermore, the whole bent of mediating theology from the eighteenth century on was toward relating the general meaningfulness of sin and redemption to the meaningfulness of a specific redeemer, so that the credibility of the New Testament records of *Jesus* as specific Redeemer had to come up. There are representatives of type 2 who take up that challenge, such as Wolfhart Pannenberg, but in the case of David Tracy, the Christ of faith does not have to be correlated with the Jesus of history; the Christ of faith is correlated instead with general human experience.

By contrast, for type 3, at least as exemplified by Schleiermacher's— to my mind unsystematic or ad hoc—correlation, that reciprocity has to be twofold: between general experience, God-consciousness, and the specific figure Jesus of Nazareth; and Schleiermacher argues that the method he builds on the phenomenon of God-consciousness can do justice to the uniqueness of Jesus as the indispensable wellspring of its Christian form. But the other correlation, between the Jesus of history and the Christ of faith, is much more problematic. In this instance, there is no clear methodological procedure for correlation, because historical method by definition cannot provide us with a person or event that is an exception to all the assumptions on which historical inquiry proceeds; it assumes that any given human beings are only relatively and not *absolutely* distinct from others. Because he wants to show the latter, Schleiermacher constantly has his Christ of faith interfere with his Jesus of history instead of correlating the two. But it is useful to point out that the reason for this attempt too was the vindication of the ascriptive literalism, not so much of the text, as of the reality to which the text referred: the historical Jesus was in fact the Redeemer.

It's a bit difficult to indicate the differences between type 3 and type 4 on these issues. Type 4, like type 3, takes very seriously the notion that in all the changes of communal Christian self-description through-out history there is also some continuity, and that the *focus* of that continuity may rest on different topics in given eras, but type 3 and 4 agree that the figure of Jesus is at the common center, certainly in modern Christian thought, and probably also in the wider life of the churches. But the means of identifying "Jesus" have been quite var-ious. There have been religious ways: Schleiermacher's experiential-religious argument employs the text for identification, but only as an outward, written expression of faith = God-consciousness. There have been historical ways: the liberal lives of Jesus tried to show both his unique messianic self-awareness and his unblemished moral superi-ority. Distinctive of the faith type is its "turn" away from the "turn to the subject" and also from the historian's quest after the "real" Jesus.

I have suggested that for type 4, unlike type 3, the "general" and the "particular" meaning under a general theory of explanation and specific Christian communal self-description are not correlated, but the first is subordinated to the second. In the description of the portrait of Jesus in the Gospels, representatives of type 4 would be pretty unequivocal about having the ascriptive subject, the specific person called Jesus of Nazareth, govern his predicates—that is, the descrip-tions in terms of which he is identified. The predicates are what they are, singly and together, because they are his, and in the way they are his. He is not simply an embodiment, not even *the* embodiment, of one or all of the predicates that describe him. (The notion of theology proposed by this type is very much oriented not only toward com-munal Christian self-description, but, like Schleiermacher, perhaps even more so, toward theology as a practical skill: we learn to interpret the Bible in order to apply it in the Church, in the secular society, in prayer, praise, and personal relation. That, I'm afraid, will not be any too clear from the small parts of type 4 I'm commenting on. But as a matter of balance it needs to be said, and also in order to indicate the proximity to type 5.)

You will recall that I mentioned the broad consensus about the priority of the literal ascriptive reading of the New Testament over any other, but also that this consensus covered only the hermeneutical level—these stories concern "Jesus" and not somebody else or no one in particular—but the *extratextual* referent or the transtextual description of this logical or literary subject varies drastically. In the modern period, there has been an endeavor to bring the two together in a "realistic" manner. The literary or textual referent and the real or true, extratextual referent were thought to be logically one and the same, largely because people confused hermeneutics, theory of meaning and understanding, with epistemology, a theory of knowledge. As a result, you had two kinds of literalists now: fundamentalists who thought that the texts as they stood were an accurate rendition of the "real" or "historical" Jesus; and liberals who thought that you had to reconstruct a picture from the text in order to get an accurate impression of the literally "real" or "historical" Jesus, although they invariably had to take certain crucial portions of the text in line with which to reconstrue the rest (the eschatological sayings, for example), in order to attain that historical Jesus. It cannot be said often and emphatically enough that liberals and fundamentalists are siblings under the skin in identifying or rather confusing ascriptive as well as descriptive literalism about Jesus at the level of understanding the text, with ascriptive and descriptive literalism at the level of knowing historical reality.

In type 4, we have a turn away from this identification, an attempt to read the text realistically or literally; but saying that, *how* one refers to it extratextually is a logically different matter. Perhaps we may want to do so analogically rather than literally, or perhaps we may want to say its truth is something else yet, rather than a matter of its corresponding, either identically or analogically, with "reality." So there has been a turn away from historical to hermeneutical ("literary" may be the best term) interpretation of the texts, a turn away from the "historical Jesus" in type 4. However one wishes to bring together the ascriptive subject of the New Testament portraits with general criteria of meaning or explanatory theory or with some specific discipline exemplifying theory, relating the Christ of faith to the Jesus of history is not the way. To the question, how do we then use the complex term "empirical" or "historical factuality" in relation to the New Testament portraits, type 4 theologians have no definite answer. Of course, they say when you do use that category, he was a fact rather than a fiction, but as the ascriptive subject of the portraits, it is his relation *to God* that identifies him, and are you seriously proposing that the relation is best specified under the interpretive category "fact"? Surely not, unless you are ready to say that "God" is a historical fact. The category "factuality" is simply inadequate (not wrong) for the interpretation of this text.

Equally, however, type 4 also represents a turn away from the subject, from the whole Kantian and post-Kantian scheme that the Christ of faith is what he is to the extent that he is it to our faith, that "meaning" is always "meaning" in relation to "understanding," to a subjective process or inner event. That turn away from the subject may imply that the text or *the* meaning of the text is regarded as simply autonomous in type 4, that is, a semiotic world of its own, regardless of its reception. At that point, perhaps one had best drop the term "meaning" altogether—as Wittgenstein and certain contemporary philosophers want us to—and use some other word or phrase, and so say that "interpretation" is making grammatical remarks about the ways in which texts are used, or interpretation is a matter of the interests we bring to the reading of texts, specifying what aims we have in mind in reading. I doubt that that would make much difference to the question. For type 4, is the text autonomous, perspicuous, and self-identical across a whole spectrum of readings? You recall that Barth had said that without some kind of conceptual scheme, some kind of philosophy or general theory, we simply couldn't read. It would be a mechanical exercise, no more than the reiteration of words. So far we are on the same ground as type 3 without being necessarily bound to "subjectivity" for providing us with that indispensable aid. There may be other philosophical tools available. Also like type 3, this representative of type 4 tells us that applying a general scheme to specific reading may well be an ad hoc affair, rather than a matter of systematic or tight correlation between text and reading, but that in order to use schemes in an ad hoc fashion, we will have to *subordinate* them to the text in the context of the self-description of the Christian community. To that end, Barth sets forth some informal "rules" for the use of conceptual schemes in interpretation of the Bible, of which the most important states:

> When the interpreter uses the scheme of thought he brings with him for the apprehension and explanation of what is said to us in Scripture, he must have a fundamental awareness of what he is doing. We must be clear that every scheme of thought which we bring with us is different from that of the scriptural word which we have to interpret, for the object of the latter is God's revelation in Jesus Christ, it is the testimony of this revelation inspired by the Holy Ghost, and it can become luminous for us only through the same Holy Ghost.[14]

To that we might well reply, "That's all very well, but now tell us *how* to apply these rules." But there's the rub, and the rub is the point. If he could tell us how, the rule would no longer be a rule but a method, a systematic and general theory for *how* to read. "Subordination" of a scheme to the scriptural text means inescapably taking a real risk, in the confidence that in, with, and under our identical or very different, indispensable auxiliary philosophical tools we may be able to reach agreement or at least mutually understanding disagreement in the reading of crucial biblical texts. We can understand—so the risk of subordination involves—we can understand more and communicate better concerning these texts (and others) than we'll ever be able to understand *how* we understand, or what the conditions of the possibility of our understanding them might be. But again, in that case, the usefulness of the theories we employ is discovered in the process of application, of actual exegesis; their use is indispensable, unsystematic, and subordinate to the text and its exegesis. The text is not inert but exerts a pressure of its own on the inquiring reader who is bound to bring his or her own pre-understanding and interests to the reading. But the relation is asymptotic. In the self-description of the Christian community, the function of "scripture" as a concept—it does not contain a "meaning" apart from interpretation or use in the Church—is to shape and constrain the reader, so that he or she discovers the very capacity to subordinate himself to it. In other words, the least that we can say is something that must be taken very seriously within the community, no matter how philosophers may view it: there can be no nonresidual reading, no complete "interpretation" of a text, not so much because interpreters' intellectual, moral, and cultural locations vary, but because a "good enough" text, to use an expression of Frank Kermode's, has the power to resist; it has a richness and complexity that act on the reader. When we disagree in our interpretations of a text, it is well to check on what each of us is doing, but it would be silly to do that and not pay attention to the features of the text or act as though it had none or as though they varied simply as our reading of them varied. In fact, we *don't* do that when we actually read and use texts, singly or together, even though we often think we do it— not when we read but when we *think* about the various ways and levels on which we read.

Barth also suggests that some biblical texts have been more crucial than others in the history of Christian reading, largely because they are more perspicuous and therefore more conductive to agreed-upon interpretation—or "plain" reading. And chief among these, so that it can serve as a kind of loose organizing center for the whole, is the story of Jesus.

When Barth turns to that story he simply follows the consensus with which we began; in fact, he confines himself to it with great care. The job of the commentator is to draw attention to the literal, ascriptive sense which serves simply to answer the question Who is Jesus in this text? In other words the commentator's task is to render a conceptual *re*description of those identifying descriptions which cohere because they are descriptions of *this* particular person, Jesus of Nazareth. Barth almost always proceeds from the priority of the singular and from the particular to the general. "Latet periculum in generalibus," he used to say, only half-jokingly. Just as he subordinated the general scheme to the specific text, in his hermeneutical priority ordering, so he reversed the logic that mediating theology had introduced in the eighteenth century and followed ever since, the logic which identified the order of belief with that of coming to believe: from the general meaningfulness of sin to that of the general notion of redemption, to the affirmation that the textual and historical individual person Jesus met the specifications of "redeemer." He reversed the flow of interpretation, claiming that the texts about Jesus were our means of access to incorporating ourselves, or being incorporated, in the world of discourse he shared with us, rather than his specific identity as Redeemer having to be fitted to the criteria of the world of our general experience.

Barth did not return to the pre-Enlightenment orthodox view that the logic of the gospel story is provided by the eternal, pretemporal scheme in which God predestines some to salvation and others to damnation, foreordaining the redeeming act of Christ in the light of the sin of Adam. Barth *did* write a long work on divine grace and predestination, but its status, despite its enormous length, is that of a grammatical remark about the language of the Gospel: Given that in the history of Jesus Christ as rendered in the Gospels we are incorporated into the reality he shares with God—and given that this incorporation is not only a *possibility* but is *actualized* in what he did for us, that his very being or essence was a being-for-us—what then is the internal logic or grammar of this depiction, not the condition of its possibility, intelligible in abstractions from it? And the answer for Barth is that the internal *logic*—if you will, the grammatical rule of this story—is the saving will of God, his election of Jesus and of us in him, from eternity. But this is a very different thing from the reverse: founding the story of Jesus on a prior and independent metaphysics of divine predestination, of which the story is only the indispensable source of information. Even here, the general (the scheme) is contained in, subordinate to, the particular (the story). It is the particularity of Jesus, enacted in and inseparable from history that makes him significant for salvation and provides the criteria for what the criteria for such significance are.

The two views, Barth's and that of mediating theology, most consistently set forth in our type 2, are well summarized in a passage from a book by Bruce Marshall:

> There seem to be two basically different and contrary ways in which the question "How can Jesus Christ be significant for salvation?" might be answered. One way would be to say that what makes Jesus Christ *heilsbedeutsam* [significant for salvation] is his own life, passion and death and resurrection, so that both the meaning and meaningfulness of "that which is significant for salvation" are determined by and inseparable from his particularity. On this account, since Jesus is *heilsbedeutsam* precisely in virtue of the actions and events which make him a particular person, principally his death and resurrection, recognizing him as the particular person he is is the one logically indispensable condition of the possibility of knowing him to be *heilsbedeutsam*, that is, of faith in him as redeemer. This position need not shun the question of how faith in Jesus Christ as the unique redeemer is credible; but

it insists that because of the way in which Jesus Christ is *heilsbe-deutsam*, this question can in the final analysis only be answered by appeal to Jesus as a particular person, and hence by appeal to an identifying description of him. On this account, therefore, the "credibility" question—the question of how faith in Jesus Christ is possible—cannot be answered by an appeal to general criteria of religious meaningfulness or significance for salvation. On the contrary, an adequate description of Jesus Christ is the logical basis of any answer to the question of how he can be significant for salvation; the task of theology in this respect is to elucidate conceptually the way in which significance for salvation is determined by and dependent on Jesus Christ as a particular person.

A different way of answering this question of credibility would be to say that in order to show how Jesus Christ can be *heilsbe-deutsam*, it must be possible to show how there can be *anything at all* which is *heilsbedeutsam*. That is, on this account one must show how it can be meaningful (*sinnvoll*) and intelligible (*verständlich*) to say that any reality is significant for salvation. Here, appeal to a description of Jesus Christ is taken to be insufficient as a basis for an explanation of how he can be *heilsbedeutsam*, although such a description is of course a necessary part of a complete account of Christian faith in Jesus as the unique redeemer. On the contrary, the general question of the credibility of that which is putatively *heilsbedeutsam* is separate and independent of the question of how the status of unique significance for salvation can be ascribed to Jesus Christ as a particular person. Unless the possibility of something "significant for salvation" can be shown to be credible, a belief like "Jesus Christ is the unique savior" will not be credible, even though a demonstration that there can be realities which are *heilsbedeutsam* does not alone fully account for the credibility of faith in Jesus Christ. Both questions must be answered in order to show how Jesus Christ can be significant for salvation; neither response by itself constitutes an adequate answer to the basic question of credibility.[15]

I spoke earlier of the fact that *if* you're not a theologian of types 1 or 2—that is to say, if you are *not* systematic in your correlation between general meaning and academic criteria and the specific self-description—you are not too worried about cutting your philosophical losses. Obviously, you don't want to talk nonsense or in flagrant self-contradiction, and, of course, you've got to try to make clear what you're after. But you won't be surprised if there's something incomplete and fragmentary about your reasoning. One way to put it is to say that you'll only be able to describe, not explain; another way is to say, as Austin Farrer put it, that the difference between a puzzle and a mystery is that whereas puzzles are rationally solved, a mystery is indefinitely penetrable by reason; another, that in this life doctrines function more like rules for talking in a Christian way, whereas in the life to come we will know how the rules are based on the very nature of things and therefore how they all fit together. I suggested that Barth did not believe the doctrine of Incarnation to be either a paradox or a contradiction but the grammar in the conceptual redescription of the relation between God and Jesus enacted in the gospel story. (The meaning of the doctrine is the story; not: the meaning of the story is the doctrine.) Schleiermacher's ad hoc correlation of the New Testament portraits with religious consciousness, with the specifically Christian mode of the more general feeling of absolute dependence, was beautiful, but he got into deep trouble when he had to relate this literally ascriptive Christ of faith to the Jesus of history. He remained hermeneutically consistent—it was the unity of the ascriptive person, God-related yet historical, that he tried to articulate—but he could not integrate theological description with historical method without effectively undercutting the latter. Barth is more consistent and, I believe, successful than any other modern theologian I know in articulating both the unity and the central significance of the ascriptive subject of the texts at the *textual* level, but he cannot specify the manner or mode in which the textual statements are historical, while nonetheless asserting that they are. David Kelsey has described the way Barth expounds the Gospels as one of treating them like a loosely organized nonfictional novel,[16] and that comes pretty close to the mark. But there is, I believe, no way in which Barth can systematically or theoretically—that is, in abstraction from examples in specific exegesis—state a general relation between textual or literary exegesis and historical statement. He will often and rightly say that textually the resurrection happened to, is a predicate of, Jesus, not to the disciples, and he will go on to say that there is no reason to think something nonhistorical just because it is *in principle* not accessible to scientific historical inquiry. In what sense, then, is the resurrection, unlike the crucifixion, historical? To consign the resurrection to the category of myth is a typical species of modern laziness or a typically lazy modernism. Schleier-macher's naturalistic view of it seems preferable! But to call it historical in a wholly Pickwickian sense is not much better, except to the extent that it is a way of saying that the inadequate and contradictory de-scriptions of the resurrected Jesus are adequate insofar as they are predicated of the literal ascriptive subject, hermeneutically or textually, but that their *modus significandi* at the level of *real* rather than *semiotic* reference remains unknown in this life and to this life's reason, and is therefore *perhaps* (!) best articulated under an analogical scheme. In the meantime, even if correlates are not available, a resurrection of Jesus remains *a* or *the* crucial ingredient in Christian discourse, under-stood, like every religious community's discourse, as a distinctive and irreducible language form. In short, Barth too, like every theologian to the right of the first two types, will have to cut his philosophical losses—not at the same point as theologians of type 3 within the general species I've called academic theology, but at a related one. But once again, for both types this may mean, if we turn this train of thought on its head, that theology is a carefully modulated way of articulating the faith philosophically but therefore fragmentarily, even though in a fit, descriptive fashion. At *some* point, though not too quickly, *philosophical* agnosticism has to set in in the interest of full-blooded Christian theology.

7 ///////////////////////////////// The End

of Academic Theology? //////

It is necessary to refer again to Karl Barth at this point. He proposed that Christian hermeneutics is a procedure whose taxonomy or phenomenology may be very simply set forth in three logically distinct but in fact united elements: *explicatio, meditatio, applicatio. Applicatio,* the last of these, is for him the transition from the sense to the use of scriptural texts. In his "rules" for using philosophical schemes or some subjective modality in reading, he was talking about *meditatio*. The proponents of type 5 may be described as saying that *at best*, understanding the Bible—and Christian language more generally—under the *distinction* between explication and application is very superficial. (The metaphor "surface grammar" in contrast to "depth grammar" is sometimes used.) For Barth it wasn't superficial, but he said that we shouldn't worry about trying to explain the distinction between explication of a text and its use in practice. But the proponents of type 5 say the difference is important because *really* to understand what religious concepts are about is to understand that concepts are—and here we should be reminded of Schleiermacher's understanding of theology as a practical form of study—verbal skills. Furthermore, the verbal skills don't exist in some mental storage house apart from the way in which they are acquired. To know the words of a specific language is to know how to use them appropriately or aptly in the specific context of that language. Communal Christian self-description is a matter of being able to use words like faith, hope, and love in the context of the Christian community—beyond it, too, of course, but on the basis of how you learned it there in worship and in the formation of Christian identity. In the words of an astute commentator on theological hermeneutics, "the concepts involved in, say, 'creation,' 'incarnation,' and 'resurrection' are not simply elements of a Christian hypothesis or world view but are ingredient in Christian life itself."[1]

When you say that in stating how they are so ingredient you refer *neither* by correlation *nor* by subordination to any conceptual scheme of an abstract or general kind, but only to the way they are acquired and practiced in this specific linguistic community, then you have type 5. "Understanding" Christian statements is simply equivalent to acquiring and exercising the skill or capacity to use them. The people who tell us these things are usually remarkable for their striking combination of single-minded integrity and pedagogical skills and force in teaching us how to disabuse ourselves of the muddle of theoretical baggage in learning the concepts. They have acquired from people like Ludwig Wittgenstein not a theory but the skill of philosophical therapy. In fact, a curious thing about them is that they often insist—rightly so—that they are not theologians, perhaps not believers, but philosophers trying to teach what religion is and what it is not. Typically, they insist that there is a sharp distinction between the language of religion and language about religion. The philosopher can teach us the differences, and (a case in point is D. Z. Phillips) what a philosopher can say about what religion is *not*, for example, a theory about whether God exists or not. But as philosopher he has to stop at the water's edge, he cannot make the transition from discussing what religion is and is not to using the language of religion itself. At that point he says, "Ask the believer and the theologian who reflects on the language from the inside, that is, by making 'grammatical' remarks about the language," in contrast to importing a general theory into it, which could make him or her only a (confused) outsider to the religion.

In using the title, "The End of Academic Theology?" I wanted to raise the question whether this procedure and this conviction didn't mean that the theologian could do no more than repeat without conceptually redescribing the words of doctrines or scriptural statements that had doctrinal overtones and aftereffects. For example, "God was in Christ reconciling the world with himself" is a perfectly sufficient saying without commentary, that is, without what Barth called *meditatio*, or saying it again in other words. But it could also be the case that there is connection of a specific nondoctrinal or nontheoretical kind for doctrinal language. An example is a little section on "Scapegoat Christology" in a brilliant recent book by Fergus Kerr, *Theology after Wittgenstein*. Referring to Wittgenstein's remarks about Frazer's *Golden Bough*, he rightly says that however rightly Frazer may have described what happens in scapegoating, he didn't realize that it was not an anachronism. "Following Wittgenstein on Frazer . . . one might be able to root the doctrine of the atonement in brute facts about the internal dynamics of any human community."[2] Well, perhaps yes, perhaps no. But in a strange way, that is, at a very concrete experiental level, we are back where John Locke first took us more theoretically: the rooting of specific theological discourse in general or universal criteria of meaning. It is a fascinating mixture: Hermeneutical silence concerning doctrine as *explicatio* and *meditatio*, and appeal to general criteria in *applicatio*—on the one hand, very close to Barth in insisting on the priority of Christian communal self-description and the practical character of theologizing; on the other, at a far, far remove from his insistence that our experience be understood in terms of the world of discourse in which God is identified with us in his self-identification with Jesus Christ, rather than Jesus Christ being understood in terms of our own world of general experience and discourse.

It does seem that here we reach at least one boundary of academic theology, as it were, from within the spectrum: doctrinal silence and acquisition of practical skills. But it seems to come to the edge from within the spectrum. This outlook seems to say: It's the pressures of internal confusion, abstractness, conceptual ineptness, and religious inadequacy within the spectrum that drive one to the edge—to reform the system from the margins. That is a very different thing from trying to envisage the end of academic theology from *outside*. To do *that* would mean trying to envisage that collapse of the present social structure of the academic theology system or spectrum and the approach of a wholly revolutionary new matrix—political, economic, and cultural— for doing theology. At the edges of imagination it is conceivable. At any rate, it might serve to make us modest.

Appendix A ///////////////////////// Theology

in the University ///////////

1. The Case of Berlin, 1810

I wish to embark on an inquiry into the character of academic theology, a species of study very much in doubt today from two sides. There are those who, upholding the ideals of genuine religion and true, passionate faith, think that it is a cold, rationalistic, arid discipline that denudes theory of praxis, Christianity of vitality, and worship of the very heart that yearns for God and salvation. Liberation theologians as well as devout, converted conservatives see in academic theology an entrapped camp follower of an intellectual elite, an alienated upper-middle-class culture, walking unsteadily on the weakening planks of a decaying First World floor. In the name of religious liberty from worldly fleshpots, and of true identification with the Christian community and with the spiritually and perhaps the economically poor—come out from among the fat ones of this world.

Critics on the other side contend that the integrity of the academy, its freedom from all intellectual authoritarianism and from all foreign institutional interference, is one of the great glories of the Enlightenment tradition of unfettered critical inquiry, and that theology has no home in its domain, for theology has neither intellectual nor institutional autonomy but bears allegiance to the polar opposite of critical intelligence: absolute authority over mind and manners, be its name Church, Bible, tradition, or Confession. The presence of theology in the faculty of a secular and religiously neutral university is an anachronism that has outlived the temporary justification it once had when Church and culture were united in the conceptual reality of Christendom; when faith appeared to be a natural relation of reason; and rational explication, the fit and natural expression of faith. It is time, they say, to dissolve the formal bond since its substance is long gone.

Neither principle nor notions of a culturally live tradition can justify its inclusion in the academy any longer.

Who can forecast the future of this embattled tradition, this little bit of flotsam on the large and churning ocean of contemporary culture? Is academic theology worth heroic efforts either of retrieval or euthanasia? I am not about to argue a case. History ordinarily does not present us with pure embodiments of ideal types in any event; it may be that in Latin America in particular, but perhaps also in sections of Africa, a new marriage will come about between remnants of the system of university or academic seminary training for the ministry, on the one hand, and communal nurture in something like basic communities, on the other, so that the old model of "theological" training for a cultured or learned and ordained professional ministry will simply relinquish its increasingly precarious monopoly. Not that it will disappear altogether, but its features will no longer define the nurture and pedagogy for Christian ministry. And perhaps this transformation will be followed by another: the successful laicizing of theology, which the academic hegemony over the subject has never seriously tried, let alone accomplished. If such a transformation be the goal of the first group of critics, it may be at least as difficult to achieve in theory as in practice. I do not wish either to champion or oppose this ambition; my aim is to draw attention to some tenacious elements in the academic tradition of theology and theological training that might either prevent such a transformation from being realized or modify it drastically at the very moment of its triumph.

Theology as a concept is closely tied to the practice of theological training and education, and both have a long history. I wish to explore some aspects of that history and what I regard as a crucial turn in its course: the transition from the eighteenth to the nineteenth century. Some historians of modern, especially non–Roman Catholic theology in Central and Western Europe and the United States (in other words, modern academic theology) have treated this territory as basically one, by virtue of shared topics and problems. Claude Welch's two-volume *Protestant Thought in the Nineteenth Century* would be a case in point, with its organization according to such large headings as "The Possibility of Theology" and "The Possibility of Christology" and its inclusion of individual thinkers, as well as national, ecclesiastical movements, under them.[1] Other historians tend to think that national or similar boundaries are the natural organizational units for this history. The chief example of this view is the monumental five-volume history of modern Protestant theology by Emanuel Hirsch.[2] (Parenthetically, it is interesting to note that few if any encompassing historical surveys of a comparative confessional or ecclesiastical sort have been written.) My own preference tends, for the moment, to be for the latter option. It may someday be possible to write histories of modern theology of a transnational or transcultural sort; indeed, that ought to be the aim of those who engage in this sort of thing, but we are not there yet. As with linguistics, we must first map out the territory descriptively before proceeding to more profound and more general interpretations. But the larger aim ought already to be visible and never out of sight. From local conditions we ought to try to draw more than local significance.

Although I intend to discuss theology in general later, I shall take for my small arena the situation in Prussia at the end of the eighteenth and beginning of the nineteenth century, particularly some of the intellectual and institutional developments that led to the founding of the University of Berlin in 1809. I shall do so, first, because the story is interesting and sets an important paradigm for other universities. The University of Berlin became the prototypical German university and the model for many others on both sides of the Atlantic. If one reads the history of Western universities in the nineteenth and twentieth centuries, one repeatedly encounters lengthy references to the University of Berlin. Negatively as well as positively, its influence was great; it was a national institution of transnational cultural significance, nowhere more so than in American higher education.

Second, there is that untranslatable German word Wissenschaft, and all that it implies for cultural and philosophical argument. I shall be using it with abandon. It has been rendered in English variously as "science," "knowledge," "philosophy," "theory of science or explanation," or "theory of reason or understanding." In German usage, it changed drastically from the vast sense that it carried at the time when the new university was being planned and begun, to a much more limited sense two generations later, when it became difficult to give the word a fields-encompassing definition except in the most formal and vacuous sense, unless of course one reserved it for one kind of endeavor alone, such as the "hard" sciences. But then, as we know, in common German usage, for once not only academic but general, Wissenschaft was never confined to the natural or physical sciences; it always included the social sciences, whether behavioral or humanistic. Wissenschaft, then, is the inquiry into the universal, rational principles that allow us to organize any and all specific fields of inquiry into internally and mutually coherent, intelligible totalities; perhaps, if we just watch our language and do not try too hard for lucidity, it may be translated as "an inquiry into the transcendental principles justifying all systematic method and explanation." Wissenschaft was the tutelary deity present—blessed and blessing—at the birth of this new university. We have lengthy essays on the character of Wissenschaft and its relation to the new institution not only from the professional sages, Fichte, Schleiermacher, and others, but even from the man in the government organization responsible for planning the university, proposing its financial base, and structuring its relation to the already existing "Akademie der Wissenschaften"—the Herr Ministerial Direktor of the section of culture and public education in the Prussian Ministry of the Interior, Wilhelm von Humboldt. Seldom have organizational, intellectual, and patriotic passions been so completely fused in the execution of an enterprise. The time was 1808 and 1809, two years after Prussia's crushing defeat at Napoleon's hand in the battle of Jena and his virtual occupation of the defeated but unconquered land. This university was owned and sponsored by the state—Germany has no civic or private universities—but it was organized around a coherent, rational ideal, encompassing all knowledge and neutral as to religion. *That* makes it interesting and important not only in the small but significant universe of higher education but in the history of theology. The philosophical faculty became, in effect, the cement and the most important faculty in the university, the arts and sciences faculty that dominated the whole; Schleiermacher, for instance, suggested that even if other, more directly professional faculties were to be included, their members ought to be legitimatized not only by their special skills but by competence in some aspect, department, or "Institute," as it came to be called, under the philosophical umbrella. Not only organizationally but intellectually, the new university was an event of importance well beyond its own borders.

The third reason for concentrating on it follows directly from the second. If indeed the intellectual idea of this university was totally wissenschaftlich and therefore secular, not only in the sense of being religion-neutral, but also of prohibiting any institutional or intellectual allegiance from inhibiting the free exercise of the critical faculty, then

Christian theology was in principle, if not in fact, in the position of having to demonstrate that it was truly wissenschaftlich and had a right to citizenship in this university. All religious qualifications for teachers and students were abandoned right from the start,[3] and the other German universities followed suit, one after another, in a very short time. Berlin was symptomatic in this respect, although Göttingen had been the pioneer. But Berlin set the pace.

We are face to face here with a double paradox. First, the Prussian state was in the throes of a major organizational transformation which was, in fact, part of the birth process of modern political bureaucracy. The reforms, initiated though not concluded under the chancellorship of Baron von Stein, streamlined the government and put each of four ministers in charge of strictly organized departments, all of them coming together under the chairmanship of the king, who in effect now shared power with his officials in a way he had never done when government was confined to his own cabinet in which he was the absolute monarch. For the most part, the machinery worked on its own, rather like the world under the sponsorship of the Deist's god. It is aptly characterized by Max Weber's notorious and frightening reflections on the conjunction of the disenchantment of our social world and the increasing fatefulness of a socially invented rationalization that displaces the responsibility of political leadership: the irresistible advance of bureaucratization peculiar to the modern Western world is "the unambiguous yardstick for the modernization of the state."[4] But in 1807, things looked far different; bureaucratization was liberation from the political feudalism of a purely personal regime.

But this rationalization was of course not democratic, even when it became embodied in a constitution. Strong residues of monarchical absolutism fused with the new bureaucratic hegemony. Prussian education was an important case in point. The organization and mutual relation between elementary schools, high schools, universities, and even the non-teaching Academies of Science became perfectly rationalized under the auspices of the Ministry of the Interior. The state possessed legal *Schulhoheit*. It was responsible for the standards as well as the administration of education below the university level and set them for both teachers and students. The state examination, not his university degree, was the high school teacher's key to being hired.[5] What was therefore astonishing was this same state's acceptance of the ideal of pure freedom for Wissenschaft in the university and the accompanying, indispensable institutional freedom of its internal self-government, the latter at least to a relatively high degree. This concordat effected with the founding of the University of Berlin rapidly became the model for all German provincial universities, or *Landesuniversitäten*. There are many qualifications to be made in this respect: for example, the prerogatives of the Ministry of the Interior in the professorial appointments process, and frequent, flagrant violations of professional privacy by a suspicious state police.[6] Nonetheless, the compact worked to the advantage of both sides, so much so indeed that German universities, especially their senior faculties, have never escaped the suspicion of governmental cooptation.[7] Each side knew a good thing when it saw one. Heavily dominated by their senior scholars, the universities became conservative strongholds after the collapse of liberal pan-German hopes in 1848. Academic freedom—*Lern-* and *Lehrfreiheit*—was not constitutionally guaranteed in Prussia until 1850,[8] when Article 20 of the first constitution read, "Die Wissenschaft und ihre Lehre ist frei." The consensus, steadily building since the early eighteenth century, that became the cornerstone of the University of Berlin and the state bureaucracy's attitude toward it, remained crucial and operative, and was once again formulated expressly in the 1949 *Grundgesetz* (article 5, paragraph 3) of the West German Federal Republic, which referred simultaneously to the legal status and the function in the context of the cultural life of the society of the concept of *Wissenschaft*: "Kunst und Wissenschaft, Forschung und lehre sind frei."[9] (The obvious difference is that in the nineteenth century Wissenschaft was considered a fixed concept, if we could only find and define it, whereas in the twentieth century its meaning depends on the contexts in which it is used and their relations to each other.)

The situation is nicely expressed by one German constitutional historian: "It is an apparent paradox that precisely the century which achieved freedom of education, research and doctrine created at the same time the greatest extreme in state direction and administration of school organization. But one can note the identical duality of nineteenth-century institutions in almost all areas; the epoch of the individual's highest freedom from the state was simultaneously the epoch of statism's greatest efficiency."[10] To a Weberian or a Marxist, this combination might not seem all that paradoxial; at least the Marxist would think that the freedom for Wissenschaft was totally abstract and confined to theory, and that the theory itself would not be a theory of praxis.

The second paradox is perhaps more serious: A Protestant Christian state, which insisted on maintaining both the traditional churches' status and its own virtually complete control of them, including control over the training for their ordained ministry, handed the monopoly for that training to the very institution, the university, which was bound to be most uneasy, perhaps even deeply skeptical, about the compatibility of such training with its own ideal of *Wissenschaftlichkeit* and the intellectual freedom and institutional independence guaranteed by the same state that governed the Church.

The Prussian state claimed a twofold prerogative in matters ecclesiastical, technically called *ius circa sacra* and *ius in sacra*. The first was the right of the government, acting administratively, to regulate the temporal affairs of the churches and their relations to the civil state. Clerical training, parish appointments, and the structure of ecclesiastical government came under this rubric. For ordinands there was an ecclesiastically administered examination, but the crucial hurdle before exercising their ministry was, for them as for other professionals, the ubiquitous *Staatsexamen*. In the bureaucratically reformed or rationalized Prussian state from 1817 on, the position of the clergyman was unequivocally that of a state official. The provincial consistories introduced in 1815 were pure state authorities that stood under the direction of the provincial *Oberpräsident*, the highest state official within the province. Under him, the consistories held state and ecclesiastic power simultaneously through government-appointed general superintendents, who were in effect their executive directors.[11] The second prerogative, the *ius in sacra*, was the right of the king, as temporal head and protector of the Church, to intervene in so-called spiritual matters: for example the shape of the liturgy and the conditions for union between Lutheran and Reformed churches. Friedrich Wilhelm III, a devout monarch, did not hesitate to enter this thicket.

The Church thus found itself in a double bind. Few people actually looked anywhere but the university for the training of parsons in the early nineteenth century, but the discomfort of the situation was clear to a good number. Ministerial training was under the complete control of the state authority, which delegated it to an educational institution whose basic intellectual and educational assumptions might well be completely at variance with those of the institution for the service of which the students were to be trained. Having been sent, as it were, by the government to the university, the theological student had to knock at the door and defend his suitability for admission not because he lacked ability, but because he was a theological student. This is the main reason why the case of the University of Berlin is the most interesting in the history of modern academic theology. It is the nearest thing to the embodiment of an ideal type; the battle over the place of theology in the academy had actually been fought out in the intellectual planning for the new university, though of course not in the administrative planning either of the Ministry of the Interior or of those academics who were their active consultants. Implicit, and often explicit, was really a double question: Is theology—and training in theology—a suitable subject for a university whose ideal is the dissemination of Wissenschaft? Or, to pose the question from the other side: Can a university dedicated to this ideal provide training appropriate to the exercise of ministry in the Christian Church? These are the critical questions with which I began. Academic theology is the fruit of this discussion.

Since that day, Christians of all persuasions, perhaps in increasing number, have answered no to the latter question. Many of them have been highly trained academics themselves. Some say that if a theory of Wissenschaft could be established for the university in which the old separation between theory and action, between speech and performance, between objective explanation and the advocacy of and commitment to social and moral change, could truly be overcome, then theology—the theory of Christian truth and action—would be appropriately lodged in a university. So, for example, one Henning Schroer, following Helmut Schelsky, proposes three kinds of *Wissenschaften*: natural sciences, historical sciences of culture (presumably this means the humanities, including textual study under some principle or principles of interpretation based on the distinctive character of understanding as the core of human being), and social action sciences (*soziale Handlungswissenschaften*).[12] All knowledge is guided by interests, in the case of theological Wissenschaft, this interest is faith and all it implies. There is a theoretical, though of course not substantive, affinity between this view and Jürgen Habermas's powerful synoptic endeavor to understand all explanation of intersubjective communication in the social sciences, and even beyond, on the basis of an inclusive theory of communicative action. But even if one wishes such ambitious undertakings the best of luck (and I do), very few people in the Western part of the First World are persuaded so far that this theory has yet come close to its goal of integrating "explanation" in the physical "sciences," "understanding" in the specifically human phenomena, and reasoning in all cases as the heuristic element of action. So far, at any rate, a real, acknowledged, and unbridged gap between theoretical language and the language of nurture for action seems to be the price we pay for the existence of relatively free and ideologically unfettered universities. *If* education for Christian ministry is inquiry mainly into the hermeneutics governing Christian action, the secular, wissenschaftlich university in which it would be legitimately domiciled has yet to be invented.

The same outcome is reached via a more direct route by those pious and forthright souls at the television street corner, for whom Christianity is primarily the nurture of communal and individual inwardness in the name of the Savior. For them, there are only a few neutral subjects—philology of the sacred languages, in particular—which they would see taught according to the ideal of Wissenschaft in a secular university. All else, including the study of Scripture and Church history, should aim at the Christian edification of the student, whereas in the name of objectivity the university teaches atheistic humanism.

Finally, there are those who have thought of Christianity largely in doctrinal or propositional terms. This is an inheritance from the Middle Ages, for which metaphysics was the purest science, and theology, whether natural or doctrinal, theoretical or practical, bore the stamp of metaphysics. Logic and transcendental principles were conformed to it, and the combination of metaphysics and logic made of knowledge a hierarchical edifice. In this outlook, the principles of the knowledge of the infinite being and revealed will of God transcend materially, even though they are formally parallel to, the principles by which we explain the existence, nature, and relation of finite things.

At the beginning of the twentieth century, a number of German Roman Catholics, using the metaphysical approach, defended theology as being a proper university subject in a debate over whether "presuppositionlessness"—that is, the indefinite revisability of all specific assumptions and conclusions, together with freedom from all value prejudice in objective inquiry—should be the criterion for the admissibility of any field of study and its representatives to the university. The great liberal academic figures like Max Weber, Theodor Mommsen, and Ernst Troeltsch (with reservations) believed in the possibility of presuppositionlessness. The Catholic thinkers argued that no coherent field of study is without its presuppositions, which they equated with axioms from which theorems are then deduced. Dogma has axiomatic status with regard to theology, and it is this intellectual status of Christian truth, not the institutional authority of the Church promulgating it, hence not even personal or valuational attachment to it, which justifies the claim of theology to wissenschaftlich status.

A modified version of that Catholic view was advanced about twenty-five years later by theologians generally influenced by the rise of dialectical theology, among them, Karl Barth, Hermann Diem, and Thomas Torrance. Theology cannot be classed under a "universally valid" concept of Wissenschaft but, like other subject matters, has its own internal logic, or, as Barth put it, its own consistent path to knowledge in accord with its own specific object of knowledge—a path of which it can render a (presumably purely descriptive rather than probative) account to anyone.[13] This is a more limited, ambiguous, and complex statement of the relationship between the universal demands of Wissenschaft and the status of Christian theology than the earlier ones, but it still certainly constitutes a rejection from the theological perspective of the secular claim to the academic omnicompetence of some integrated, universal form of reason in a transcendental mode. Whether on the basis of Christian faith as a form of action, as inward experience of religious meaningfulness or salvation from sin and evil, or as doctrine or belief embodying the true knowledge of God, there were Christians deeply skeptical for religious and conceptual Christian reasons that a university dedicated to the ideal of Wissenschaft could provide training appropriate to the exercise of ministry in the Christian Church.

The same doubt had been expressed with at least equal force by the academics. In the traditional view, Christian theology was regarded as simply incompatible with instruction in a university dedicated to the ideal of Wissenschaft. The argument to this effect was spelled out by the philosopher Johann Gottlieb Fichte, but it had already been prefigured by Kant, whereas the ecclesiastical opponents of the arrangement found no distinguished advocates until the beginning of this century. In his essay entitled "The Quarrel of the Faculties" (1798),

Kant had attacked the traditional primacy accorded to the theology faculty.[14] He contrasted the three higher faculties (that is, theology, law, and medicine), which are founded on statutes rather than reason, to the philosophical faculty, which is accountable for the truth of its teaching and must therefore be "free, standing only under the jurisdiction of reason, not of government." The three higher faculties have usefulness as their aim; that of philosophy serves truth. Theology must uphold biblical teaching, whereas philosophy is free to subject biblical faith to the critique of reason. Fichte went further along the same road.[15] "A school," he writes, "of the scientific use of reason presupposes that whatever is given to it may be understood and penetrated down to its ultimate ground; accordingly, something which proscribes the use of reason and puts itself forward *a priori* as an unfathomable mystery, is in the nature of the case excluded from such a school."

If theology insists on a God who wills anything without cause, the content of whose will no human being can grasp through his own capacities (*durch sich selber*) but only through direct, divine communication by way of special emissaries; if it insists that such a communication has taken place and the result set forth in certain sacred books ("which by the way are written in a very obscure language") on the correct understanding of which the human being's salvation depends, then a school of the use of reason can have nothing to do with it. Theology will have to admit candidly "that the will of God can be known without special revelation and that these books are in no way a source of knowledge but only a vehicle of popular instruction, which, quite independently of what the authors *actually* said, must for actual use be explained in accordance with what the authors *should* have said, which in turn—as they should have said—must therefore be known apart from and prior to their own explanation."[16] Shades of the Deist controversy from the time of Toland's *Christianity Not Mysterious* or—shades of Kant's biblical hermeneutics in *Religion within the Limits of Reason Alone*! But because the argument centers on organizational and not merely intellectual concerns, Fichte goes on to state that theology, like the other two higher faculties, includes an element belonging not to the scientific "art" (*wissenschaftliche Kunst*) but to the "art" of the practical, and he associates the surrender of the privileged status of mystery or revelation with the separation of theology's practical from its scientific part. The reasons for this coupling are not entirely clear, but seem to be based solely on a common negative: neither practical skill nor revelation is science. Give up the claim to privileged knowledge of God together with practical instruction in the ministerial arts, and you may include theology in Fichte's plan for the university. Theology's territory would be divided up among philosophy, history, and philology. No hankering after the inclusion of praxis in his notion of theory. The issue is strictly intellectual: Reason versus revelation as a test for university membership, with revelation meaning pretty much what it had meant in the earlier eighteenth-century debates, even if the concept of reason had been transformed from the rationalists' universally applicable analytical and critical instrument to the idealists' vast, universal, and unifying Absolute, ingredient at once in the world and in consciousness. Fichte is in the happy situation of affirming that universal reason without mystery is actually equivalent to religion.

But the matter of practical theology would neither surface nor disappear. Fichte had excluded it from philosophy, or the domain of reason, but it was by consensus of church leaders an inalienable part of clerical training, and not a mere concession to the folk customs and psychological needs of "the populace" (*der Volk*), as Fichte put it rather condescendingly. (Remember David Hume's pleasure in the use of the term "the vulgar.") He saw the practical work of the parson simply as that of a people's schoolteacher, mediating between them and the scientifically educated. ("There is no higher level than the scientifically educated," Fichte said in a revealing phrase, "and what is not *wissenschaftlich* educated, that is the populace.") As a matter of fact, the absolutist Protestant principalities of preindustrial eighteenth-century Germany had assigned the clergy precisely this task of popular education; Fichte did not pick it out of the air. But the Prussian educational reform measures signaled a drastic change: a nonclerical professional teaching class was developing, and it encompassed all the stages of the system, from elementary schools through the universities, their collective self-awareness held together as much by their status as public officials as by the astonishing contagion of the educational principles of the Swiss educational reformer, Johann Heinrich Pestalozzi.

Schleiermacher's *Speeches on Religion to the Cultured among Its Despisers*, perhaps the most influential religious manifesto of modern times, should be read as much as a manifesto of professional as of spiritual independence from the feudal social conditions under which the educated cleric as well as other professionals of *Bildung* had been laboring. For him, unlike Fichte, the state was always as much the potential threat to as the benevolent supporter of an independent, free university as well as a free church, and that meant that both clerics and university professors had to guard as best they could the distinctive status and dignity of their professions. Schleiermacher was a feisty political liberal. The strongest theologian in modern Germany until Karl Barth, he wanted to dignify the professional status of the clergy. In a rather dismaying phrase, he characterized the clerical church leader as "a prince of the church." The best one can say about this portentous phrase is that it may be a sly way of denying that title to the king in a Protestant country in which it might otherwise have gone to him by default in the absence of an apostolic hierarchy. Schleiermacher specifically included the union of the wissenschaftlich enterprise of theological inquiry with the professional, practical exercise of the parson's profession under the pretentious title. But how were they to be kept together? Clearly, Schleiermacher would have to argue for the importance of practical theology—or theology, at least to a significant extent, as a practical discipline—against its denigration by Fichte: and since Schleiermacher consented to the model of state university monopoly in the education of parsons, he had to argue for the appopriateness of practical disciplines in the university structure. He developed the argument for theology as a practical skill or discipline in a monograph entitled *Brief Outline on the Study of Theology*,[17] and the argument for the admissibility of theology to the university in an essay called *Occasional Thoughts about Universities in the German Sense; Together with an Appendix about One Newly to Be Constructed*.[18] They are nearly contemporary works: *Brief Outline* was published in 1810; *Occasional Thoughts about Universities*, in 1808.

Brief Outline is the most distinguished and influential representative of a certain Continental, especially German, eighteenth- and nineteenth-century genre called "theological encyclopedia," intended to set forth to theological students and others the coherence and perimeters of theological education, its unity and its diversification into special subfields. Schleiermacher's monograph sets forth the aims of theological education, its method or methods, and, unlike some others of its kind, its relationship to other fields within the university, but always from the perspective of theology as an integral discipline. *Occasional Thoughts about Universities* proceeds from the other direction. To the extent that it touches on theology and theological education, it does so, as it were, from without, examining the reasons for including theology in a secular university plan. The actual structure of the University of Berlin turned out to be far closer to Schleiermacher's ideas than to Fichte's both in general and in respect to theology in particular.

Schleiermacher, like Fichte, gives philosophy the preeminent place among the faculties. For Schleiermacher, philosophy really contains the "idea" or essence of the university, and as with Kant and Fichte, philosophy is equated with Wissenschaft in general. Schleiermacher is more rigorous than Fichte about distinguishing between transcendental or formal philosophy—the universal and certain principles of explanation that apply to all special fields and their justification; the explanation of the condition of possibility for any and all knowledge—and material philosophical systems that lay claim to actual, informative knowledge of reality, specifically, of metaphysical reality. That is because Schleiermacher, unlike the other idealist philosophers, believed that the union of thought and actual reality is a goal toward which we may steadily move, but which is never actually attained. No true philosophy can claim certain knowledge, but only one-sided, identical systems. There is no intellectual transcendence, intuitive or discursive, of the subject-object duality, but only a preconceptual one. Hence, the statement of the conditions of the possibility of knowledge (he used the term *Wissen* to indicate a more comprehensive noetic state or act than specific, positive knowing, *Erkenntnis*) is at once detached from all specific subject matter and yet unreal except in relation to it. Transcendental possibility and actual, empirical reality are logically distinct but in actuality always given together.

Further, in rather cautious and limited agreement with Fichte, Schleiermacher holds that the transcendental condition of their actualized unity includes more than such logical principles as coherence, character of truth assertion, meaningfulness of descriptive statements, and so on; it also includes a self-involving perspective on the totality of things natural, cultural, and transcendent: a *Weltanschauung*. The idealist view of Wissenschaft, in other words, included or presupposed a whole-making outlook that served at the same time to justify that universal validity. Here was a claim to a comprehensive unity of all specific knowledge which at the same time insisted that each specific area had its relative autonomy—a comprehensive unity at the same time cognitive or noetic, aesthetic, and moral, based on a conviction of the unity, accessibility, and self-accessibility, or privileged status, of the human subject in its relation to all else. This privileged unity meant that the relation between subject and object was always in some way interior: we interiorize the world of knowledge as well as art and morality, so that education is at the same time edification and character nurture: Bildung was the German word for the process, and it combined a philosophical vision of solidly founded, unified knowledge (philosophical idealism) with its inherence in a view of humanity as a unique and privileged reality vis-à-vis the rest of the world (German historical scholars call this latter view *Neu Humanismus*). Even the inherited tradition of religion as special revelation found its niche in this tidy system. To the extent that it could be interpreted into the more basic terms of the system and did not claim to be an ultimate source but only a means of knowledge, it was rationally meaningful and admissible to status within a philosophical faculty.

But suppose this complex view of the unity of Wissenschaft collapses and with it the philosophical anthropology of human being as distinguished by self-consciousness, to which it is so intimately related, so that, at least arguably, neither one can exist without the other? In the context of this work, one would then have to raise the further question, What happens to the status of theology in the university when each particular science becomes a tub resting on its own bottom, with only the thinnest or most formal relations among them, such as the criteria of logical coherence; specifiability of standards of meaning and character of truth assertion; freedom from arbitrary, imposed, and non-revisable axioms; and non-interference in conclusions from the side of normative value judgments (a grave suspicion hanging over the idealist view of Wissenschaft)? These were the elements of a later stage in the quarrel between Wissenschaft and theology, when a more positivistic view of Wissenschaft had taken the place of idealism. It was then that the debate shifted focus to the presuppositionlessness, rather than the rationality, of science versus the constraint on conclusions and non-revisability of premises of theology, rather than its irrationality, mysteriousness, or mythological character.

The concept of Wissenschaft changed, while its legal status remained the same. It was *free*, however it was defined, in 1810, in 1850, and in 1949, in Prussian and German constitutions. But whether or not Christian or any other theology can qualify under its rubrics and therefore claim its protection within the university becomes an increasingly complex question as the interpretation of the concept, philosophical or other—Wissenschaftstheorie—becomes increasingly problematic. I do not need to stress at Princeton the problematic character of the issue whether or not philosophy is a or the foundational discipline for others, to which they must appeal for legitimation. Nor do I have to stress, in this particular august department, that potentially negative arguments concerning philosophy as a foundational discipline do not go very far toward reestablishing theology as a legitimate university discipline. I am not here to argue a case. The point is that the decision on that score may finally have to be made on other than systematic philosophical grounds: on the one hand, legal-institutional; on the other, cultural. Does one preserve a tradition within a significant cultural institution when that tradition threatens to become culturally anachronistic? Who or what body has the right to decide? Is a charter enough to go by? Suppose the charter at some point conflicts with the guarantee of academic freedom?

The University of Berlin was founded in a context in which Christian theology was not, even though it threatened to become, *culturally* anachronistic, in part because of the close relation of intellectual and social life in this middle-class culture, and because in that culture, secular modernization and Protestant tradition tended to fuse harmoniously. But the legal status of theology and theological education was safe, because the Church was an official part of the state and the state likewise owned the universities. Academic theology was therefore twice blessed, if that is the right word.

For Schleiermacher, the issue of theology in the university was more complex than it was for Kant, Fichte, or Schelling (Hegel in this, as in most matters, is an obscure question). On the one hand, he was a full-blooded Christian theologian who would not countenance the reduction of theology to philosophy; theology is an independent discipline. On the other hand, he acknowledged that philosophy—especially transcendental philosophy and not a system of supposedly positively informative philosophy—is the essence of the university. In a nice summary of his view in *Occasional Thoughts*, he stated that the business of the university is to teach the young to "regard everything from the point of view of Wissenschaft, to see everything particular not for itself but in its nearest scientific relations and insert it into a wide common frame, in steady relation to the unity and totality of knowledge, so that they may learn in all thinking to become conscious of the basic laws of Wissenschaft.[19]

On the one hand, Schleiermacher agreed with Kant and Fichte that

the three so-called higher faculties—medicine, theology, and law—
were included in the university by reason of tradition and social usefulness rather than intrinsic relation to Wissenschaft. He thought they
were, in a word, professional schools that taught a special skill and
sometimes threatened (especially in the case of law and divinity) to
degenerate to the status of trade schools unless their faculties also
qualified in some philosophical—we would say, liberal arts or science—department. The so-called higher faculties were not really of
the intellectual essence of the university. They were special or specialty
schools, *Spezialschulen*, which the state had either founded or at least
taken under its protection because they related to its essential needs.
They originated "individually from the need of founding an indispensable practice through theory, through a tradition of *Kenntnisse*."[20] By
contrast, the philosophical faculty, because of the purely rational rather
than social or pragmatic nature of its work, ought basically to be seen
as a private partnership by the state, over which the latter has no
fundamental but only a secondary social authority. Schleiermacher
agreed with von Humboldt's striking statement of the conditions for
the flourishing of Wissenschaft: solitude and freedom. They are also
the conditions for Bildung, cultivated learning for its own sake and
thereby for the sake of personal enrichment or development.

On the other hand, this lofty view of philosophy and its free status
did not imply for him, as it did for Kant and Fichte in particular, either
a denigration of the professional school or the illegitimacy of its presence in the university. The university is an institution in between the
Academy of Sciences, with its specialized and pure research, and the
school, with its straightforward instructional aim. (Hence the rationalistic title of his essay.) The German university, unlike French and
British institutions of higher learning, mediates between the two and
partakes of the character of each. The specific aim of the University of
Berlin at its founding was to unite teaching and research in its activities
and its organization, Schleiermacher said, and he spoke for all. But
this goal also meant that training for the public professions, and not
only instruction in the arts and sciences, could claim a right equal to
that of Wissenschaft in such a university, not only by appeal to ancient
university tradition but also in and of itself. The consequence is that
the *actual* university cannot consistently embody a single, coherent *idea*
of the university. To those who worry over this eclecticism, Schleiermacher simply replies, "See if you can come up with anything better

before you scrap this proposal." His view won the day resoundingly. But that in its way is startling. Here was *the* university, the conception of which was most deeply influenced by a philosophical system, the idealist view of the rational and unitary character of study; the university, furthermore, that was to be the model for others in Western Europe and the New World. And it, of all institutions, found itself, from the start, unable to embody its own unitary idea, while the man who ended up defending both—the idea of the intellectual unity and supremacy of Wissenschaft and the university, and the actual as well as conceptually irreducible diversity of the institution of higher learning—was himself one of the leading idealists. It was a triumph of orderly eclecticism over system by a leading systematician. And he based the right of theology to a place in the university on the status of the ministry as one of the professions in the modern sense.

In the light of Schleiermacher's advocacy of the proper place of the professional faculties within the university, let us look briefly at his description of what they do. Their instructional activity, unlike wissenschaftlich instruction, stimulates an intimate connection between theory and praxis, but it is interesting to note that Schleiermacher does not propose a theory for their connection. The professional schools are there because of "the need to found a (socially) indispensable practice through theory, through a tradition of *Kenntnisse*." In context as well as lexicographically, that rather flexible, many-sided term suggests what we would tend today to call the acquired skills, the font of information together with the conceptual skills that go into the mastery of a field. Obviously, the "theory" referred to in this rather awkward sentence is not the high-powered explanation of the conditions for the possibility of the practice; rather, it is more like the grammatical remarks that further us in the use and informal reflection on the rules of the use of a language we are learning, to appropriate the language of the later Wittgenstein and his little flock. What about the theology faculty specifically? It "was shaped in the church in order to preserve the wisdom of the fathers, in order to distinguish truth from error—as already in the past—and not allow it to be lost to the future, in order to provide a historical basis, a nice and definite direction and a common spirit for the further development of doctrine and of the church."[21] So far, then, theology is a "positive" enterprise that is neither transcendental philosophy nor specific method linked to a universal, philosophical foundation, but the acquisition and impartation of the continuing tradition of a community—an ecclesiastical culture, if you will—by means of the proper use of its language under conditions of cultic continuity and social change.

Of course, theological training employs "scientific" history; but it is from beginning to end informed by a sense of history that scientific history cannot supply and may not even be able to warrant, a sense of that continuity of language and custom which we call "tradition." In terms we have been taught in this century by people like Clifford Geertz, Paul Ricoeur, and even the deconstructionists, what Schleiermacher was saying was that a tradition is the acted text which is the performative language of its members. Theology is the conceptual redescription of that text and also the grammar of that redescription—that is, the testing of that second-level language for adequacy to the text or to some privileged element in it, such as Scripture.

In *Brief Outline of the Study of Theology* and later in his dogmatics, *The Christian Faith*, Schleiermacher develops the same view as in *Occasional Thoughts*, but this time from the point of view of theology, showing how Wissenschaft (philosophy and history in particular) is appropriated within that enterprise. He was absolutely consistent in the parallel between instructional context and its organizational structure. Just as the organization of disciplines in the university is eclectic, so the relation between Wissenschaft and theology is one of correlation that never becomes identification, even though one may specify principles or modes of awareness and thought that define the harmonious relation and interaction between these two ways of using language for technical purposes on the same set of topics.

In *Brief Outline*, Schleiermacher speaks of theology as a positive science or discipline (Wissenschaft), and defines that term as follows: "A positive *Wissenschaft* in general is a compass of scientific elements which do not cohere as though they formed a necessary part of scientific organization in virtue of the idea science, but only to the extent that they are required for the solution of a practical task." And the task of theology is indeed practical: "Christian theology is . . . the compass of those skills [Kenntnisse, once again] and practical rules [*Kunstregeln*, rules that are the fruit of practical skill rather than theoretical deduction] without whose possession and use a cohesive direction of the Christian church, i.e., a church government, is not possible."[22]

What is striking about this view of theology is not so much its admitted elitism ("prince of the church"), or even its evident academic

character, but its *professionalism*, and, in that sense, its skilled, specialized, practical character. Theology has always been an almost if not
fully official part of the Christian religion, one of its defining elements
in a way that may not be nearly as true of other high religions. But in
Schleiermacher's hands this connection reached its apex. I believe he
both articulated and embodied an actual state of affairs. This was true
in two convergent ways. First, he claimed the irreducible specificity
of Christianity at the primary level of a "mode of faith," a cultural-
religious tradition, and a linguistic community. Second, he claimed it
as the second level of the language of the community in expert hands
for the practical aim of organizing the skills of governance.

One way of stating Schleiermacher's correlation between philosophy
and theology in the university—between the language of the academy
and the Church—is to say that the language of the academy is explanatory, whereas that of theology in the service of the Church is
descriptive. Schleiermacher thought that in the disciplines outside the
physical sciences, conceptual description had been up to then as basic
as explanation by subsumption of specific phenomena under general
laws and general laws under a comprehensive conception of knowledge and being. He was, in fact, looking for a nonreductionist dialectical relation between descriptive and explanatory modes in what he
called the science of *ethics*—that is, culture and history—which would
do justice to the nonrepeatability and individuality of phenomena and
to the distinctiveness of their description from the agent's or exper-
iencer's point of view, while at the same time permitting not only
appeal to patterns of similarity but to lawlike causal connections between sequential human events and social structures. Theology for
Schleiermacher was obviously related to the universe of thought and
discourse under general rules of coherence, meaningfulness, and faith.
But it was also context-specific; whatever else may be true of wissenschaftlich thinking, theological thinking is a conceptual skill governed
by practical aims. It is meaningful discourse not only to the extent that
it is coherent but also to the extent that its meaning is simply the
intelligent discourser's or agent's social aim. Theology is as intimately
and basically explained by a sociology of knowledge as by a philosophy
of the knowledge of reality. In fact, to the extent that Schleiermacher
advocated the primacy of the practical aim ot theology within the
Church, the nearest external discipline to it is a social science that
describes, and in describing explains, the way theological language

functions as a part of the web of relations constituting the community of which it is a part. A nonreductive sociological or anthropological understanding of the acted text constituting that culture, together with its first- and second-level discourse, is the external equivalent to theology—not identical with it, but an appropriate external explication of it.

The social sciences were not invented yet and thus formed no part of the new university's table of organization, but Schleiermacher had an equivalent for them; he called it *ethics*, which is theory of culture and within it philosophy of religion, which is actually the comparative study of organized religious communities, including Christianity. Schleiermacher gave powerful expression to it in his comments about the aims of theological education. He exemplified it in his life, and he represented what was then a still recent but already typical reality in academic theology, the significance of which has not been sufficiently explored. Professionalization means expertise over a given field, through governance of the information pertinent to it, and even more through the distinctive methods of understanding and dealing with that information. It is an expertise over which legally and socially acknowledged rights are exercised by the experts themselves. They set the standards of membership, usually through a group organization regulated by public authority. The person's expertise is the source of his or her livelihood. Not only are the practice of law, medicine, and the ministry prime examples of professions backed, privileged, and regulated by public authority; in the bureaucratic Prussian state, holding office in the bureaucracy became a profession. University professors were state officials; they became professionals both because they were experts and because they were officeholders in the public, governmental domain. In contrast to New England in the early nineteenth century, following the disestablishment of Congregationalism, where the status of the ministry changed from public office in the community to profession, in the Prussia of the Reformation at about the same time, *Amt* and *Beruf* converged. Theologians were university professors. By virtue of their status and their specific expertise, and because they were trainers of budding members of the same calling, they became members of a profession that virtually came to define their identity. They were *theologians*, rather than divines or learned men who taught theology. They were simply professionals, just as we have intellectuals, novelists, licensed beauticians, and therapists today. There is a whole culture of professionalism, and in regard to theology, Berlin led the way.

2. Types of Academic Theology

The tension that Schleiermacher exemplified between theology as *Wissenschaft* and theology as an activity of the Church continued—indeed continues—to haunt both theology itself and theological education. Three generations after Schleiermacher, Adolf von Harnack, the great historian of Church and dogma, refused to give up on the two sides. In a notorious discussion with Karl Barth, he insisted that theology must continue to be scientific.[23] Its claims about God, Jesus, and history must be warranted by objective, scholarly investigation, and its beliefs about the meaning of faith and life in the Kingdom of God must be continuous with the tradition of cultural and humane ideals inherited from the past. Harnack did not despise practical theology, the nurture of leaders in the Christian community, but he clearly saw it not as the *aim* of the whole program of theological study but as a kind of derivative, secondary craft. In principle, the person who had mastered the *scholarly* disciplines of the theological curriculum and participated in Christian community life already knew what there was to know about the pastoral and homiletic arts. Harnack, however, played a leading role in the rejection of the proposal to transform the faculty of theology into a faculty or department of the science of religion—not merely for Berlin but for the whole of Germany. Berlin remained the paradigm. He was, after all, the leading liberal voice, and if he declined this essentially liberal or radical proposal on the part of those who considered theology simply not compatible with the ideals of objective scholarship, then it had no chance at all. It seemed to Harnack, as to many other liberal theologians at the time—only Ernst Troeltsch was eventually to turn his back on the conviction—that Christianity really illustrated the perfection, or the most complete embodiment, of the genre religion. Therefore, if you studied the Christian religion, you studied religion in principle. The only thing you lacked were the requisite languages, which should be studied in other parts of the university. Departments of religion encourage dilettantism, Harnack thought. But beyond that negative reason for retaining the theological faculty, he insisted positively that education for the pastorate was something that could not be surrendered by the university.

This part of his argument, however, tended to be isolated for two reasons. First, he could not really give any significant content to the professional aspect of the ministry and training for it. Second, the very notion of religion, including Christian religion, had for him an intellectual or moral-spiritual essence. It was not really the kind of complex organism which had to be understood as a social and cultural artifact, a continuous and constantly recreated structure in its own right. It was not necessary for it to be understood that way, because that was the periphery, not the heart, of religion. So Harnack, unlike Schleiermacher, defended the distinctiveness of Christianity and the right to existence of the theological faculty on grounds that really led in the opposite direction—toward the non-distinctiveness of Christianity and of training for the pastorate—in cultural outlook, in basic method, in the understanding of religion. Harnack upheld Schleiermacher's policy without Schleiermacher's understanding of the need to correlate two very different academic aims and procedures. He believed in upholding and passing on a tradition, but he did not assume that we share the convictions and problems of our predecessors in that tradition. Harnack's way of putting it was that Paul and Luther and, yes, Herr Kollege Barth too, can never be the subject but only the object of study for one in the academy. Right there, hermeneutical inquiry was rejected in favor of historical method—and, at least at one level, this was the essence of the quarrel between him and Karl Barth.

For a "hermeneutical" stance, whatever else may be said about it, means that you share intellectually the world of discourse you are studying, that it becomes the text of which you are a part in understanding it, no matter how you apply it and to what extent you may live in another language domain in other respects. Like its great deniers, conceptual analysis and deconstruction, hermeneutics takes seriously the textuality of the text, whether it is written or enacted as a community, a culture. For Harnack, the ideals underlying theology were completely identical with those that gave birth to the University of Berlin: the ideal of humane culture as the aim and sole common hermeneutical context for study; the ideal that the only way to realize *this* ideal is the pursuit of strictly objective study, which meant in effect historical study. History, for Harnack and for many others, was *the* archetypal discipline.

Whether the two ideals are compatible or not is a question for another day. What one must note, I think, is the enormous problem of trying to maintain the distinctiveness of Christian theological training when one denies the distinctive character of the theology. Harnack simply passed up the issue and the necessity for establishing coherence between the intellectual and social structure of Christian (or any other coherent culture, for that matter), and therefore coherence between language about both structures. He both intellectualized and spiritualized the Christian community. Although Schleiermacher was tempted in the same direction, he did not travel down that road nearly so far. But the lesson of their differences is highly instructive. In the wake of the modern university tradition of academic theology, certain formal patterns of intellectual organization have become basic in a way that had not been known before: the organization, aim, substance, and method of the study of theology made the relation between Wissenschaft and theology the fundamental determinant for harmony and conflict among theological schools of thought. In other words, one can arrange a typology around the answers to this issue.

Obviously, there can be other ways of organizing the field. Where theology is not professionalized, where method does not govern substance to the same extent, its options may look different. But wherever appeal is made to the public character of the understanding informing theology—that is, to a generally intelligible hermeneutics—there the Berlin tradition rears its ugly head, demanding that theological instruction and its organization do justice both to church training and to principles of general explanation that hold for all disciplines; demanding, furthermore, that some sort of coordination or correlation be effected between the two, be it a correlation between autonomous, distinctive ways of thinking and speaking, or some attempt to locate the rightful status of the one through the priority of the other, or a claim that the two are in principle absolutely different and there can be no real contact between them.

Schleiermacher clearly held the view that church training and *Wissenschaft* were autonomous equals, while Harnack asserted the priority of scholarly learning over practical theology and, unlike Schleiermacher, understood the social setting, organization, and character of theology as adventitious to theology as a theoretical, purely intellectual discipline. For Harnack, both the relation and the distinction between theology and other academic disciplines was simply a matter of reflection on the principles of unity underlying and warranting the diversity of those sciences, and the focus of theology was not so much the study of religion as of history, which was all but sufficient to give us the normative as well as descriptive essence of Christianity. Schleiermacher was searching for a dialectical resolution of the tension between theory and practice, Wissenschaft and theology, state university and Church, autonomous human culture and obedient Christian discipleship. Harnack, like his colleague Ernst Troeltsch, saw no tension there because the first partner in each pair had priority in principle over the other as genus has over species; but, unlike Troeltsch, he was confused over the matter because, like Schleiermacher and unlike Troeltsch, he wanted a distinctive status for the second in at least one case; theological training was to be autonomous and therefore independently organized from the university scheme governing all disciplines claiming access to public and general rules of description and explanation. The status of theology in a university like that of Berlin should have appeared far more precarious to Harnack than it did, because, unlike Schleiermacher, he saw no difference in principle between theology and the faculty of arts and sciences.

How basic a quarrel is this? Can one really construct a typology of theology based on various outlooks toward the organization of the university and on the theory that there is a right relation between theory and practice which is at least potentially embodied in the organization of the university? Certainly, I do not claim either that it is the only possible way, or even an exhaustive way of organizing the field of theology in the modern West, to say nothing of the South or the Third World, or of churches as different as the Roman Catholic and the Pentecostal. Perhaps, like other such organizing enterprises, it is not a structure independent of but relative to the aims for which it is constructed. Its relative adequacy will be no greater than the light it casts on certain topics, generally admitted to be significant and enduring over a period of time and discussion, such as, for an example, the question of the meaning of Jesus Christ for believers and for the world at large, which has been carried on over the last 150 to 250 years.

The other way of testing the basic character and significance of this kind of typology is to ask whether it is fair to see other ways of distinguishing between kinds of theology as secondary and variable to this one, and that also is a difficult matter. Can one claim, for example, that process theology, neo-orthodox theology, liberal or revisionist theology, evangelical theology, liberation theology, deconstructionist theology—and all those other theologies that succeed each other at breakneck speed—are best viewed under this organizational instrument rather than as independent schools of thought to be compared in their own right? The answer again will depend on a number of factors. For example, liberation theologians frequently invoke the term "hermeneutics" to indicate a general view on the relation between theory and practice under the priority of the latter, and then authorize biblical interpretation under this view, demonstrating the amenability of the Bible's contents to the understanding with which they approached it. How serious is this hermeneutical stance? To what degree is it independent of the exegetical results? How open to counterclaims or revisions at the level of theoretical generalization? Or, conversely, how open to revision is theory if its application results in exegetical puzzlements? If, by these criteria, liberation theologians are serious about the hermeneutical theory and are not simply using it in the interests of an independently established explication and application of the Gospel, then despite their severe critique of academic theology, we are still in the channels charted by institutions like the University of Berlin.

There may well be theologies of which one would have no more than a poor caricature if one described them in terms of the dialectic between, or range of types from, those that insist on impeccable consistency in method to those that advocate consistent self-limitation to discourse about a distinctive mode of life. The proponents of such theologies never went to school in nineteenth-century Berlin, and the academization and professionalization of theology didn't happen to them, and bully for them. These issues may not arise, at least in this form, for Third World theologians, or for those who skipped the Pietist and Enlightenment transformations of theological education, for whom theology is still first of all the contemplative and devotional habit of the mindform of the knowledge and love of God, and second, the use of the trained intellect in penetrating that abiding mystery. (Austin Farrer's Bampton Lectures, *The Glass of Vision*, come to mind.)[24]

But despite such qualifications and caveats, the *problematic* and the span of theological possibilities represented by Schleiermacher's so-called mediating theology, embodied in the arrangements in the universities patterned after Berlin, are our concern. The extreme ends of the spectrum are represented by two positions that cut the tension which Schleiermacher wanted to maintain between them (or their early-nineteenth-century equivalents) thus reflecting a basic ambiguity in the status of Christianity in the modern West. Christianity has been viewed and has viewed itself as an independent religious community characterized by certain ritual forms and institutions, a common Scripture, communal memory of Jesus of Nazareth as its founder and the image of God, a set of cultural attitudes in which compassion is prominent, and so on. It has also been seen as an official or at least privileged institution in the general cultural network of social and intellectual attitudes and arrangement—the residual, if often increasingly tenuous and residual, religion of Western culture. The two views are not necessarily in conflict; they may perhaps be combined; but they are certainly distinct.

In the second view universities are the higher educational representatives of the culture, and if theological education is admitted through their doors at all it must be under conditions common, or at least demonstrably not contrary, to the rules for academic disciplines in the institutions of higher learning in this culture. Those rules are, as we have seen, academic freedom from all extrinsic authority and loyalty to public, generally valid, intersubjective modes of explanation (Wissenschaft, once again), as well as to the justification of such explanations (Wissenschaftstheorie, or Wissenschaftslehre, as Germans call it).[25] In content, not only modes of explanation (Wissenschaft) but their justification (Wissenschaftstheorie) have continued to change drastically since the acceptance of the idea, but the rule remains, even in the absence of anything like consensus in regard to its substance.

The most vigorous and continuous argument has been between those who believe that distinctively human phenomena, whether of individual or social life, are subject to a different kind of explanation from the lawlike explanation of natural and physical phenomena, those who deny it, and those who believe that one can show continuity between the two without affirming the identity of explanation in the two kinds of cases. For all three views, however, the formal description of the mode of explanation, or its nearest equivalent, that is applicable to the particular class of phenomena, is held to cover at least the whole class, so that the pertinent procedure can be stated apart from any given instance of its application. So, for example, *hermeneutics* (the term is a prime instance of the fact that one word may cover a multitude of completely different sins) is used often in the wake of Wilhelm Dilthey to describe a coherent structure for understanding any and all manifestations of meaningful human activity. By reason of this generality and its consistency, *hermeneutics* is taken, at least by those who believe in it, to qualify as Wissenschaft, even if it is more nearly descriptive than explanatory, confining answers to the question *why* to agents' reasons for their actions rather than to causal laws explaining types of behavior.

Because theology in the general academic tradition under discussion has generally been thought to have a stake in the distinctive, irreducible character of human consciousness—extending the term even to characterize the life of communities, nations, and cultures—theology has been considered to have a special affinity with hermeneutics; by some it is actually thought to be an instance of hermeneutical procedure. Such is the character of explanation or explanation-equivalent ("interpretation") that theology offers. The particular phenomenon that it interprets, or for the intelligibility of which it accounts, is that situation or mode of understanding called revelation or disclosure. Hermeneutics is only one example of an affiliation for theology that will, if accepted on both sides, allow theology some kind of wissenschaftlich standing. Clearly, no matter what *particular* discipline may be the affiliate, theology finally ends up being affiliated to it by virtue of that discipline's general rational structure, its independence of any "positive" fields that assemble and interpret specific data. In other words, the affiliate to theology is some form of transcendental philosophy—even if not in the original, heavily idealist sense of that term. That is what makes theology at least a presentable candidate for admission to the university.

It is only natural that under these auspices the term *theology* is used generically, just as philosophy itself is. "Christian" theology is one instance of the general class or generic type, the classification for which came into being with the turn from the Enlightenment to its various nineteenth-century successors, and it is the general class—including the specific examples—that must be subsumed under general criteria of intelligibility, coherence, recognizability of its particular form of truth assertions, and so on, in order to be recognized as a university discipline. Its right to that place of dignity depends on its exemplifying criteria of validity under general Wissenschaftstheorie. This is the heritage of the tradition of academic theology under the governance of Fichte, and of Schleiermacher too, to the extent that he explained theology as the conceptual quest for the description of the essence of some particular mode of faith and recognized philosophy as the essential, underlying discipline of the university.

At the opposite end—though *opposite* is an awkward term here, since we ought not to assume at the outset that the two positions are pure contrast cases—theology is an aspect of Christianity instead of a generic discipline under which Christianity is included. Theology, in other words, is religion-specific. Whether or not other religions besides Christianity have theologies, or something like them, would have to be adduced case by specific case, and one would have to try to see in each case what the depth of the commitment of the community to that kind of enterprise was over a long period of time. If I may recall an impression of my own: Because of early Jewish-Christian theological arguments, like that of Justin Martyr's *Dialogue with Trypho*, it did not occur to me for years that not only was the Jew in that interchange a straw man (that was easy enough to see), but the very mode of conversation, description of and arguments for and against conflicting truth claims in the two traditions, was far more characteristic of Christian than of Jewish religion. Jewish writers were more apt to develop theological concerns when they were in strong contact, friendly or hostile, with other cultures and religions—for example, in the twelfth and nineteenth centuries—than at times when Judaism was more inwardly focused. One would have to ask if the sort of reflective energy, largely but not exclusively borne by an intellectual elite, that went into theology in most Christian groups, went into an equivalent but different activity in Judaism. Is Midrash the theology-equivalent of Judaism? Or, vice versa, is theology the Midrash-equivalent of Christianity? Suppose that were the case—both the parallel and the difference between the two might be instructive.

One often hears arguments as to whether one can make significant generalizations about the internal logic of Midrash, or whether it is more nearly an exegetical art with typical formal moves like those to which Robert Alter recently drew attention. A puzzle or a kind of gap in a biblical verse is stated; next, reference is made to verbal or semantic parallels in parts of the Bible distant from the original verse. With their help, one returns to the original verse, often with something like an element of surprise connection—hence the temptation of post-structuralists to see Midrash as an instance if not a paradigm of intertextuality—and so covers the hiatus between verse and problem. There seems to be general agreement among the Rabbis that the literal sense takes priority over any other in this operation (at least until Kabbala), but this seems to be more an insistence on sticking to the recognized range of use of specific biblical words than a self-conscious appeal to a logical or other, wider frame for interpretation. What the Rabbis agree on is not generally as ambitious as, for example, the rule that interpretation covers in three aspects, explicatio, meditatio, applicatio, or the distinction between varieties of nonliteral senses. Midrash is unlike Christian theology but may well fill a similar function: showing the community how to use its sacred text, and doing so through the instrument of a kind of instruction that has continuity of form. In each case, the ultimate recipient of instruction is the community, and it is equally true that in each case the instructional activity is itself communally sanctioned. The method of instruction is in each case one of defining the elements of that religion as a semiotic system, and we might say after Max Weber that rabbis and theologians are ideal types. The mode of instruction employed in each case is in the service of the tradition.

How does theology function in this view of it as Christianity-specific? It is first of all the first-level statements or proclamations made in the course of Christian practice and belief. This religion has characteristically had a strong communal belief component set forth in creeds and confessions, though one ought not to go so far as to think of those as *the* "essence" of Christianity. But second, theology is a given Christian community's second-level appraisal of its own language and actions under a norm internal to the community itself. This appraisal in turn has two aspects. The first is descriptive: an endeavor to articulate the "grammar," or "internal logic," of first-level Christian statements. The second is critical: an endeavor to judge any given articulation of Christian language for its success or failure in adhering to the acknowledged norm(s) of Christian language use.

Let me cite an instance of both. The Chalcedonian affirmation, authoritative in traditional Catholic and Protestant churches, states that Jesus Christ is a single, unitary person in whom are united perfectly (not, so to speak, synthesized) two complete, unabridged natures, human and divine. The formula has two functions. It is first of all an assertion; it is a judgment that "this is so," and in that sense a first-level statement. But it is also a second-level statement descriptive of the internal logic that went into the formula, with a critical appraisal implied. It was the response to two unacceptable proposals: one (the Antiochene) doing justice to the fullness of the human nature, but not to the unity of the person; the other (the Alexandrian) to the fullness of the divine nature and the unity of the person but not to the fullness of the human nature. The formula sets forth the requirements to be observed in the employment of these Aristotelian-Platonic categories in an identifying statement about Jesus Christ. Any statement that would deny the full humanity, full divinity, or full unity of Jesus Christ is unacceptable. In the form of a rule, the statement is negative, setting the limits beyond which no such identifying statement can go.

But we can put the same second-level function more positively. The formula is a conceptual redescription of a synthesis of the gospel stories understood as the narratives identifying Jesus Christ. It is taken for granted that in that story he, the protagonist, is a unitary agent, so that, whatever the relation generally between the categories "person" and "nature," in this case they both function logically as descriptions of the unitary subject to whom they are ascribed. The logic, I suggest, of the formula is that of a subject-predicate description, rather than that of substance-accident description. That does not mean that the *ontology* or metaphysics implied is of a subject-predicate rather than a substance-accident character. The philosophical conjunction of subject-predicate logic with subject-predicate ontology did not take place until Hegel. At the descriptive second-order level, the substance-accident metaphysics is in the service of the subject-predicate logic. The "grammar" of the formula, I suggest, is that the subject to whom predicates are to be ascribed, the unitary ascriptive subject, has a certain priority over the descriptive characteristics that he embodies. They are *his*; he holds them and is himself as each of them singly and both together. I shall return to this theme, for it suggests what I take to be the root way of using the literal sense, which in various forms—it is not a univocal term—has been the basic rule for biblical reading in the Christian community.

The basic use of the literal sense is ascriptive rather than descriptive; it is descriptive only in a secondary way. *That this* subject—none other; not no one; not everyone; not two, one fleshly and one spiritual; not a personified quality or set of qualities—is the subject of these stories, is the basic, literal affirmation, which I find echoed theologically, that is at the level of conceptual redescription. The logic, then, of the formula as redescription is that of a priority of the statement of the unity over that of the duality, but at the same time it maintains that this rightful priority of the categories' (divine/human) unitary personal ascription over their abiding logical distinctness and unabridged character must not jeopardize the integrity of the latter. It is to be noted that the internal logic is inherent in, perhaps even limited to, the case; no statement is being put forth here as to the general conditions of intelligibility that would make this statement possible. The statement of the formula's logic is not of a transcendental, at least not of a strongly transcendental, kind. Nor does the formula affirm that Christology must be thought about in ousia/hypostasis categories. What is at stake is the proper identification of the agent under a categorial scheme, not the correctness or indispensability of the scheme: the meaning of the doctrine is the story rather than the meaning of the story being the doctrine. That is why if one thinks about Christology in a non-narrative fashion one must do so in a carefully limited, ruled sort of way.

Back to Berlin and the two extreme poles of our budding typology. Theology in the first sense has philosophy for its natural cognate discipline, especially transcendental philosophy, and because transcendental philosophy claims to provide the theoretical justification of all explanation (Wissenschaftstheorie), theology is accountable to it. In effect, it is a subdiscipline of philosophy which provides it with its criteria of meaning and truth and, of course, with its academic organization. No matter what theology may entail logically in practical consequences, it is vocationally the profession of an intellectual, a theorist.

Theology in the second sense is a practical discipline; it is in effect part of learning the grammar of a linguistic symbol system; it is Christian self-description under some norm for its specific language use. No matter what it may entail logically in matters of theory, it is part of the praxis, the ruled practice of culture, part of social tradition enacted by a participant, an agent who knows how to use the language in its appropriate context. The formulations of the Christian confessions and their interpretations may be taken that way.

One sobering question, to which we will not be able to give an unambiguous answer, is the extent to which the agent is necessarily also a professional. Traditions do change, and social patterns that religions find peripheral or even compatible in interaction with the surrounding social world in past eras, they later reject as going against the grain of the tradition under changed circumstances. Slavery, the ordination of women, the institutional rigidification of the ownership–wage earner structure of industrial and postindustrial capitalism become, each in its day, issues to confront the ongoing tradition of the appropriate service of a Lord who would be a servant, who is equal and not superior to the least of his brothers and sisters, and in whom—so it was recognized early on by at least some of his followers—there can be neither East nor West, slave nor free, male nor female. A professional class—in the full modern Western sense of a typical aspect of rationally organized, bureaucratically governed societies—is surely not inherently part of the notion of that theological office or teaching activity which does seem to be built into the Christian tradition.

The question is further complicated by the fact that no matter how incompatible, or even incommensurate with each other, the two distinct ways of conceiving theology may be, they were both embraced by the culture of professionalism. The Prussian state legally granted independent professional status to the intellectuals by recognizing their right to non-interference in the exercise of their expertise, and employed them as members of the state bureaucracy. The theologian was thus a professional both as an intellectual, a *Wissenschaftler*, and as an instructor of church professionals sponsored by the state. The question we cannot answer clearly is the tantalizing one: To what extent are the very thought patterns of our theological types a function of this common organizational pattern; to what extent is ours a typology of theological professionalism? Should the arrangement disappear, will the conceptual types disappear also, concept being part of a form of life?

Clearly, theology of the second type or group is more amenable—in principle, though not always in fact—to this kind of question than the first, whose own Wissenschaftstheorien (theories of what is involved in explanation) are likely to be exempt from subjection to the social relativism which its proponents sometimes attribute to the theories of other groups.

A strong relation of theory to practice, of language to social structure, of explanation to sociolinguistic custom, is more apt to be affirmed by the second than the first group. The naturally affiliated external discipline for understanding what Christian theology as second-level descriptive and critical appraisal of its own language and actions under a norm internal to the community itself may resemble social science more than philosophy. Concepts are taken as problem-solving devices in the quest of individuals for living together in coherent groups. They are not, however, simply species of individual behavior but socially embodied rational acts, to be understood through the uses to which they are put in determinate contexts. They are not secret mental events taking place in back of their public manifestations, but shared conventions under common rules—and in that sense rational—which we call symbol systems. The rules governing these networks of communication are for the most part implicit, not because they obey an anterior logic that can be separably specified, but because they are context-dependent and vary in accordance with the uses that they illustrate. The substance of the rules is the illustration rather than an independent explanatory power inherent in them.

It is as true to say that language is a form of action as to reverse the statement and say that any action may be read as mode of speech. But the paradigm for intersubjective communication still seems oral—perhaps, par excellence, the dialogue. Yet dialogue itself could not be carried out except under antecedent linguistic conventions, objectified in institutions that range all the way from documents to parliaments and ethnic cuisines, and therefore it seems better to vary the metaphor and say that action is a text to be read, rather than an oral communication to be listened to. To say that it is a text is to take away a dimension of mysterious "meaning," a ghost in the machine which, rather than its semiotic structure, would constitute the text. In addition, to say that action is a text is to accent not only its location in the public domain but that, more than oral communication, it is fixed, at least long enough to be read, and fixed because of its communal dimension, the antecedent conventions that enter into it. To be meaningful, any action must be both conceptually informed, on the one hand, and in accordance with the structures that are its condition, on the other. While we might be tempted to give precedence to the second criterion, we do so at the risk of reifying it; we might be tempted to give precedence to the first, but in that case we not only atomize actions but tend to mentalize them. When we use terms like culture, symbol system, or, in our case, a religion as a symbol system, we had best think of both together, intentional action and social structure.

Yet that seems very difficult to do, once we ask how to combine them. There are theorists of social science who stress the role of intentional agency in the public or cultural domain, whether they do so linguistically like Peter Winch, or more eclectically like Clifford Geertz.

In the case of Winch, the descriptive task of understanding an action under its governing concept seems all, and explanation under generalizing theories that would allow structural comparison within and among cultures disappears. For Geertz, explanation is added to description, but, I take it, only weakly. The reverse is of course true of structuralists of all kinds, including Marxian structuralists like Louis Althusser, who excludes the ascriptive subject together with intentional action as a basic part of the social structure to be explained. Then there are the critical theorists, people like Habermas, for whom the descriptive aspect, the distinct hermeneutical operation of understanding rather than explaining, is part of the social scientist's task, which acknowledges the integrity of understanding rationally conceived action. But the hermeneutic operation of understanding the agent's concept in context must be included in a larger theory that not only overcomes the traditional separation of an understanding of the reasons for human acts from an explanation of the structure and causes of behavior, but also enables the social scientists to "assess critically the structural arrangements of social life."[26] That is to say, critical theory wants to overcome the separation not only of understanding and explanation, but also of fact and value, which was part of the value-free positivist program for the social sciences. At the heart of critical theory is the coherence between the factural and normative assessment of the structural constants of the basic, unvarying forms of all social arrangements: language, labor, and domination.

But to return to our subject, Schleiermacher's inability to integrate conceptually the idea of the university and the practical school of professional education, together with the state's championing of clergy education in the university, left us with two concepts not only of theological education but of theology. In the first, theology is not only affiliated with philosophy as a transcendental discipline or theory of explanation that assigns to theology its criteria for scientific validity but is ruled by philosophy. In the second, theology is affiliated with the social sciences. But some caveats need to be observed. First, unlike the relation of theology to philosophy in the first case, in the second the relation of theology to the social sciences is much more nearly *external*. The Christian theologian uses the concepts that inform the Christian community and, in using, describes them; the social scientist describes or understands them without using them; and the difference, one of practice and judgment, is of course important, even if conceptually hard to express. Second, and here is the purpose of the digression, social science as practice, at least as the practice of social scientists, bears a stronger family resemblance to Christian theology in our second sense than much of social science theory. Where that theory is detached from the practice, it is most apt not to be autonomous but to become an aspect of philosophy as general explanatory theory—Wissenschaftstheorie, once again. If that happens, of course, theory of explanation in social science turns from being a flexible, open-ended thought experiment to a much more basic outlook in which generic continuity or discontinuity between the social sciences and the physical sciences becomes a matter of life and death. And then you either agree with "formalists" that there is strong continuity, based on the formal identity between the structure of explanation in any rational endeavor that claims to be scientific (there may be other uses of reason, of course)—that is, you agree to the "reduction of the singular to an instance of a (universal) law"; or you agree with "contextualists" that since *all* explanations are theory-laden, we must address their pragmatic setting and communal functions, instead of analyzing their formal structures.[27]

The continuity between natural and social science thus consists of the same absence of formal continuity in both areas. Theologians, at least of the second kind, are almost invariably followers of Thomas Kuhn in this regard. It seems natural enough, but one wonders if they haven't made too heavy an instrument of the family resemblance between social science and theology when they opt that way. The relation between the two remains external, and most congenial for theologians whenever theory leaves room for intentional agency and subject-predicate talk, no matter how, in a logically separable move, they may want to place such talk explanatorily. A lot more may be done to develop the similarities between theology and social science in practice than a justifying theory of explanation may warrant. So much the worse for the theory. I still think that Max Weber's classic *The Protestant Ethic and the Rise of Capitalism* is a model of just that kind, fitting by means of the ideal type of the Protestant vocational ethic of inner-wordly asceticism, a pattern of belief and action into a broad social structure, so that it becomes part of that structure and part of the causal explanation for its transformation—and Weber does this without giving up on the irreducibility of understanding, without confusing reasons and causes, and without attributing causal efficacy for the rise of Western capitalism and the middle class to this factor alone.

For the theologian of the first type, insisting on theology as Wissenschaft, brought up in Berlin, there were or are no such worries over distinguishing between and relating an external and an internal description of religious symbol systems, so that all else—ritual, ecclesiastical patterns—are only the external signs of religions; they do not constitute it. For this theologian, theology is a fit subject for study in a university like Berlin only if its special beliefs and moral codes, the appeal to mystery or authority, embodied in an obscure book, are cast aside. In other words, specific religions may be studied in a university and a faculty hired for that purpose, to the extent that they can be understood as positive, historically specific expressions of beliefs and morals based on universal reason, reason here constituting reality and human consciousness and the bond between them. For the theologian of the practical kind, each religion is a distinct social structure and each has a language of its own that cannot be reduced to an aspect of a general religious language—a language expressive of the category "the sacred," for example—though of course there may well be overlapping features among religious institutions such as ritual, forms of verbal symbolization, authority structure, interpretive procedure, and so on. To understand that distinctiveness of structure and language is a hermeneutical task, that is, a task of understanding the religious symbol system as both a written and an enacted text, through a kinship between internal and external description or redescription, ambiguously related to each other and, in the first case, to truth claims, but in the second, to theories of explanation. For the second type, there has to be a distinctive hermeneutical element or moment for the distinctive character of the religion to be understood; in other words, it cannot be done by historical or philosophical means alone. There is for the second type no sharp separation between conceptual and social description. The fact that theology was a purely academic discipline is important for the second as well as the first kind of theology, and for their notions of theological education. The fact that theology was increasingly regarded as practical rather than theoretical knowledge from the later Middle Ages on was also important for both outlooks. But the fact that theological education in the university was organized along both intellectual, academic and professional, practical, institutional lines makes little difference to the character of theology and its relation to theological education in the first view. But in the second, it is intimately related to the conceptual account of the religion, including the place of theology and theological education within it. The institutional aim of the latter and its professional character are part and parcel of the content to be understood, not merely a practical by-product or basically distinct context for the content of theology, which is intellectual belief and revelation, experience, or whatever that belief is based on and which it symbolizes. The hermeneutical or conceptual dimension and the social-scientific one in the description of the religion are closely linked.

But these clearly are ideal types in a certain, partially Weberian sense. Some of their characteristics are exaggerated and one-sidedly presented. They do not often appear in pure shape in actual theological proposals, although it seems over the last 175 years of academic theology that the first achieves pure embodiment more often than the second. But that is precisely why there can be an actual typology of academic theology.

Appendix B ///////////////// The Encounter
of Jesus with
the German Academy ///////////

It is frightening to stand behind a lectern or sit in a comfortable seminar room and talk about Jesus Christ. It is incongruous. Surely among all those who have been accorded the stature of Savior or charismatic leader by their own religious groups as well as others, he is the most demanding from the vantage point of lectern and seminar room. Discipleship to him has often been a joy to those who have pledged it, but equally frequently it has been a joy under the guise of great unhappiness, if one is to believe a remarkable consensus of Christian testimony. "If any man will come after me," states one text (Matt. 16:24) imperiously, as New Testament texts so often do, "let him deny himself, and take up his cross and follow me." Many people become the followers of Jesus when grief brings them into his company, and their lives are transformed in unexpected ways: they discover the ability to endure, or an unsuspected capacity to be surprised by joy. I would guess that few altogether worldly or fully contented people are Jesus' disciples. He is a very demanding figure—to judge by a large consensus in a long tradition—requiring both our confession of him as Lord and Master and a form of life not indeed heroically reiterative of his own but recognizably shaped in his image even though at the distance of imperfection.

Part of the summons to Christian life is the inquiry, "Who is this man?" but it is striking that even someone who says that we can no longer answer that question in any meaningful way still finds the link between it and the summons to discipleship compelling, and finds that that link is not established by us but by Jesus. Albert Schweitzer could accept neither a traditional ecclesiastical nor a modern liberal description of Jesus, nor was he satisfied for religious purposes with the picture of consistent eschatology for which he himself had argued as a historian. You doubtless remember those powerful closing lines of *The Quest of the Historical Jesus*:

> The names in which men express their recognition of Him as such, Messiah, Son of Man, Son of God, have become for us historical parables. We can find no designation which expresses what he is for us.—He comes to us as One unknown, without a name, as of old, by the lake-side, He came to those men who knew Him not. He speaks to us the same word: "Follow thou me!" and sets us to the tasks which He has to fulfill for our time. He commands. And to those who obey Him, whether they be wise or simple, He will reveal Himself in the toils, the conflicts, the sufferings which they shall pass through in His fellowship, and, as an ineffable mystery, they shall learn in their own experience who he is.[1]

These words are not only haunting in their thrust to the precipice where eloquence and inarticulateness meet; they are also sternly demanding. Whether one agrees with their author's religious stance or not, they convey an authentic force.

Yet we ought not to push that compelling severity too far. There are also no doubt many ways in which his yoke is easy, his burden light (Matt. 11:30). The *analogia fidei*—as our theological ancestors used to call what they saw as the agreement among seemingly diverse, if not discordant, parts of Scripture—is an operation we ought to carry out, though with restraint. We ought not to appeal to his imperious call to a difficult discipleship without also remembering that profound humaneness manifest in the texts that has attracted so many followers to him—and of course vice versa. The specifics of a sketch of his teaching as well as his being remain incomplete and fragmented, and their cohesion in interpretation, as I said, a matter of restraint: Complete or nonresidual interpretation of any text, but especially of a combination of juxtaposed texts, is a tempting but elusive business. Jesus is a very specific person as he emerges from the fragmentary and diverse fourfold description in which he is rendered for us, yet in that variety there is also the claim of unity which allows people of great diversity access to him, and him access to them. It is not surprising that, more than other savior figures, he has called forth any number of fictional redescriptions, which start out from apparently very specific individual character features and broaden those features out until the figure finally takes on universal scope and becomes the representative of all humanity.

There is something very specific about the original portraits. In all of them he is recognizably and clearly himself and none other, and yet the specifics are fragmentary if not at times contradictory, so that they move strangely, if not by constant counterdescription (such as abiding personal power and equally abiding powerlessness), toward an all-encompassing universality. Look, the portraits seem to say, he is none other than *a* person, *this* person, and yet unlike any other, he is—or is representative of—all persons, humankind as such. Even the abiding contrasts Jew and Greek, bond and free, male and female (Gal. 3:28) are encompassed in the universality of this specific person—yes, this *man*—though no other person, male or female. When Christians want to describe human nature, they do not proceed, like philosophers, by abstraction, by generating the universal or the general out of its particular instances. They do not proceed even like historicists who combine the particular and the general by describing the ideal type or unitary cultural consciousness of a specific culture and era— a kind of generalized particular. No, they look to this man, as though true humanity could never be explained, never be generalized about or abstracted from concrete, specific description, but as though the description of this specific man, like all good fictional description, included far more than this person—in fact, the whole race, each one of us in her or his specific and different being, doing, and undergoing.

To say "like all good fictional description" is not to deny Jesus' historicity but to express great skepticism over the historian's—rather than the novelist's or dramatist's—capacity to generate a *character* portrait of him in which concrete, non-idealized, unified particularity is all-encompassing universal human being at the same time. To express skepticism about the historian's ability to do what the fiction writer does, to read the portrait or portraits of Jesus, is to follow a different hermeneutical rule from that of the historians, or, rather, to follow a *hermeneutical* (in a broad sense) *rather* than a *historical* reading of the text. Karl Barth once said simply—and for him, unusually briefly— "the gospels are testimonies, not sources." David Kelsey in turn said that Barth read the Gospels as loosely structured nonfictional novels.[2] Wayne Meeks recently termed the Gospel of Matthew a messianic biography.[3] To read hermeneutically is to read with greater caution than reading historically, because the unity in the portrait will be more complex.

Speaking of that complexity, I stated earlier that we ought not press the severity of Christ's demand too one-sidedly, because his compassion is equally great. The wife of a theologian of my acquaintance, a man single-mindedly dedicated to his work, said to him one day: "You didn't really become fully human until you stopped being totally preoccupied with Jesus." I think a Christian case can be made that we have not met the textual Jesus until we have also met him, as Søren Kierkegaard said, in forgetfulness of himself or incognito in a crowd. Perhaps the most haunting identity statement or identity description of Jesus in the New Testament is Matt. 25:40: "Inasmuch as you have done it unto one of the least of these my brethren, you have done it unto me." Who is the Jesus of this text? He is that Messiah, that Son of Man, who is not *identical* but *identified* with the poor, the undeserving, the spiritual and economic underclass. They may not know it, there may be more of them who would laugh rather than be comforted by it; but according to the text, it remains true that he is that Savior who walked incognito—you recall that neither the sheep on the right nor the goats on the left recognized him—in the midst of these least of the underclass. He was self-identified with them, though he was neither identified by nor identical with them.

But that is probably not all my colleague's wife had in mind, nor is it all there is to that humaneness of Jesus that allows us to counter his compassion and his severity with each other. You recall the saying from the Sermon on the Mount (Matt. 5:24): "First be reconciled to your brother and then come and offer your gift (at the altar)." Perhaps nothing is more miraculous than the fact that ordinary kindness and natural gentleness can be the earthly form taken by that divine love (agape) which is so utterly disproportionate to the ordinary. The enjoyment of the neighbor in her and his peculiar character, religion, lifestyle, and work—the enjoyment of just the way she or he is—may also be part of the service of Christ: Reconciliation as a form of celebrating co-humanity—or, less ornately put, loving the neighbor as oneself—seems to be what the text recommends before we come to serve God or his Christ in the specific place set up for the purpose ("before the altar"). Because of this textual Jesus' inclusion of *all* humanity, in all its variety, in himself, we have known disciples of this kind also, who love their neighbors and take a simple pleasure in them—all sorts and conditions of them, the dispossessed and the disadvantaged, but not only them—for their own sake and do so not compulsively—not, as it were, hounding them with the image of Jesus—but with simple and delighted generosity. In a religion touched by such apparently contrary marks as severity and generosity and a Savior so specific yet so universal, so particular and yet irreducibly potentially exponential for almost every kind of human quality, the line between devotion in religious service and fanatical religious imperialism can be thin, but it is real and deep, and a generous unobsessive love of the neighbor marks that line.

The foregoing discussion of that complex simplicity which characterizes the portrait of Jesus in the Gospels, and its inclusion of all humanity within itself, may bear a certain resemblance to what such theologians as Nicholas Lash and Colin Gunton agree is the rather unfortunately named "Christology from below," which begins with the man Jesus and moves from some distinctive feature in him or his message to his distinctive and final or insuperable status and the unique presence of God in him. Yet the exegetical sensibility that he includes all human nature in his specificity is much more reminiscent of the *anhypostasis* and *enhypostasis* of Alexandrian Christology, the proposal that in him Godhead supplied the specificity for that generic humanity which he had assumed, than it is of Wolfhart Pannenberg's ("from below") proposal that the resurrection of Jesus be argued as the historical confirmation of his teaching and as the link between empirical-historical inquiry and theological interpretation in regard to Jesus, and that one go on from there to theological claims.

I propose instead that we turn to a kind of minimal but important agreement in the history of the Church about the text of the Gospels which, by a kind of gradually attenuating extension, has covered the text of the New Testament and from there also the text of the Old Testament. I refer to the priority of the literal sense (or reading) over other readings of the text. Except for the Reformation and thence the modern period, other readings have always had a legitimate place in Christian reading of the so-called canonical scriptures. By and large, they have not been systematically integrated with the literal sense, but simply *subordinated* to it: Within broad limits you may do as you please, and the consensus is that the rule governing how you interpret is religious or edifying rather than literary. Scripture must be interpreted, and it may be interpreted as you wish as long as the love of God and neighbor is enhanced by how you read (as Augustine, for example, stressed), or as long as nothing unworthy of God is read out of the text (an important criterion for Origen). The technical subordination of spiritual to literal reading was loosely coordinated with such material guidelines. Obviously, they could not prevent conflicts in the content of actual exegesis, or even among competing guidelines themselves— the vigorous debate between Alexandrian and Antiochean schools of interpretation is eloquent testimony to this fact. Still, by and large, a consensus kept reemerging in the West to the effect that the literal sense had at least a limited priority over allegorical, moral, and ana-gogical senses, so that *Jerusalem* might indeed designate the eternal city in the heavens toward which all the creation hastens, as well as the Church that is the bride of Christ, and the soul that longs for him— but not at the cost of dissolving the reference to the specific town in the Middle East.

Qualifications have to be made almost all along the way. Beryl Smalley tells us that at the beginning of the Middle Ages some form of spiritual rather literal reading was given priority in monastery schools and that the literal sense did not reassume first place until the Victo-rines.[4] The literal sense itself undergoes transformation (there are apparently no less than four meanings of it in the late Middle Ages). In the Protestant Reformation, it becomes the equivalent of grammatical and historical reading at the same time—to the exclusion, as far as possible, of all other readings except the figural reading, which is itself a kind of extension of the literal sense. In the Enlightenment period, the literal sense begins to be transformed into something it never was before, an outlook which at the beginning of the twentieth century became known as fundamentalism and included a strong evangelical element. (Evangelicalism could take either a theologically liberal or a conservative direction; it did both in Germany, England, and the United States.) Fundamentalism identified the grammatical and liter-ary sense of a text with what the text's words ostensibly referred to. *If* a text was not poetic or clearly metaphorical and was of a descriptive character, then clearly it must be either factually true or false. To paint with too broad a brush, we may say that it was possible before the eighteenth century to read texts literally and at the same time leave the referential status of what was described in them indeterminate. Especially if God was described, the principle of analogy could be invoked, so that one could say, "We believe this is a true description, even if we do not know the mode of signification in which it applies to God." Such complexities were gone soon after the beginning of the eighteenth century, when concepts like "fact," "probability," and "verification" turned all language into a mirror of reality or a perceptual report of our knowledge of what is extramental. It is, I think, a fair description of the earlier outlook on language, including the literal sense, to say that it affirmed that we have reality only under a description: that reality, the extramental world, is not language-neutral. But once empiricist philosophy, Deism, and the first glimmerings of historical criticism appear on the horizon, all that is changed, and the literal sense now becomes simply a likely or unlikely factual report, and factual reporting is language's foremost function.

The most obvious candidates for vehement controversy after this development, of course, were miracles—descriptions of events in which God supposedly intervened directly in the causal sequences of nature and history, or events that went counter to our uniform experience: the six-day creation and the resurrection of Jesus from the dead preeminently. The Bible—rather than being the "grammar of the Holy Spirit," as Luther had once called it; the inspired Word of God; the written source of the presence of the living spirit to heart and mind—became *either* a source of supernatural information that was at once factually and doctrinally true or false, *or* simply a particular channel for transmitting general knowledge that was available in principle without it.

My reason for rehearsing this familiar bit of history is to try to address by means of it a rather different if equally familiar question: What is the essence of Christianity? theologians and historians of this and the last century have asked. Professor Stephen Sykes in his Cadbury Lectures[5] addressed the issue and indicated that there is no single answer (it is an "essentially disputed concept"), but that elements of answers were possible if we look at the parts that theological controversy, the principle of inwardness, and theology as a power principle have played in the history of the Church. Without questioning this subtle and persuasive analysis, I wish to raise the question whether one cannot reach some degree of agreement on certain matters of content also, and that these have to do with the curious, even if at times distorted persistence of the literal reading of the Bible I have been describing and with the relation between such reading and the place of Jesus in the religion. It may well be quite fair to assert, as many people have said, that when it comes to doctrine (not necessarily the most important part of Christianity, but certainly an inalienable aspect of this religion), the faith of the Church in premodern times tended to be Trinitarian rather than simply Christological, and that the marked sense of Christological concentration in modern theology was a function of the controversies over the credibility of a supernatural revelation in the eighteenth and nineteenth centuries. Even so, few will doubt that Jesus of Nazareth has in all ages been at the center of Christian living, Christian devotion, and Christian thought. In all the diversity of Christian description about Jesus, obviously the text of the Gospels has been our primary resource. Even if we are historians who think that the real historical figure has to be reconstructed from the texts, we will become literalists at some point and say, *here* the text and the actuality coincide. In other words, what fundamentalists say about the *whole* text of the Gospels, liberal historians say about a *few, selected, and crucial* texts: the crucifixion perhaps, certain ipsissima verba, some of the parables of the Kingdom, some eschatological sayings. In any event, at some crucial points concerning Jesus—where they believe the description and the true history coincide, or the description becomes a genuine clue, so that what Jesus was truly about truly emerges there—liberals become at least minimal literalists in the modern sense.

The consensus that I think I see, tenuous and yet constantly re-emerging from the earliest days through the Enlightenment period into the twentieth century, East and West, North and South, is that of the priority of the literal sense in regard to the texts concerning Jesus of Nazareth, chiefly the descriptions in the Gospels, but to some extent also in the rest of the New Testament. It is a very simple consensus: that the story of Jesus is about him, not about someone else or about nobody in particular or about all of us; that it is not two stories (most people abandoned the supernatural features of the story rather than concede two stories) or no story and so on and on. This does not mean that there are not other legitimate readings also: for example, readings in which we the readers are included in the text, or readings in which Jesus shares the spotlight with the Kingdom of God or with universal religious experience or with some specific quality which he embodied, such as love or moral reason or faith. But the general consensus has been that Jesus has primacy in these stories.

One may speak in terms of such a broad consensus only in regard to the *hermeneutical*, and not the *reality* status or reference, of the gospel accounts. For example, one might assert, at least in theory, that the reality embodied in this story is that of a general state of affairs of which the story is an historical, fictional, or partly historical, partly fictional illustration. Or one might claim that the reality embodied in the story is that of eternal Godhead assuming individual historical shape. One might also say that rather than describing or illustrating either a particular or a general state of affairs, the story expresses, symbolizes, evokes, or reevokes experiences beyond telling and the power of words, except indirectly. Some of these claims may be more compatible with what I called the hermeneutical consensus than others, but as long as one makes the logical or categorical distinction between the hermeneutical and the reality status of the story or stories, the two need not be in logical contradiction with each other, no matter how infelicitously by any given set of criteria for doing so the two may be yoked.

Not until the late eighteenth or nineteenth century were serious attempts made to schematize or systematize the literal reading of the texts as Jesus' story with one of the other readings, so that they were both at once; by and large until then their relation simply had the shape of an informal rule, not of a conceptual system or unitary structure: every reading was legitimate as long as it acknowledged that it was secondary to the literal reading.

But three qualifications to the compass of this consensus are necessary. First, the literal sense is focused on the story of Jesus Christ. Indeed, it seems to me—I can take bold and illegitimate liberties since I am not a historian—that a case might well be made that the literal reading of Scripture in the Christian tradition is virtually organized around this story, that the reading of Scripture becomes in a loose and not fully aesthetic sense a *literary* literal exercise, unlike (for instance) Midrash in Jewish tradition, for which a similar primacy of the literal reading is much more nearly a syntactical and lexicographical rather than literary exercise, in which possible options of biblical verbal uses are carefully explored and compared.

Second, what is "literal" in the literal reading and becomes the "plain" sense—that is, the closest thing to consensus—is not in the first place the description of Jesus or the titles bestowed on him or the like. No, the literal sense is in the first instance very specifically focused on him as the specific, unsubstitutable personal subject of the stories.

This is a difficult matter, and some technical categories are unavoidable. The relationship between Jesus in his story and what he says, does, and undergoes is a deeply intimate one: his identity is not *illustrated* but *constituted* by these things. He is not a logical substance unchangeably posited behind his qualities and deeds, as it were accidentally related to them. No, he *is* what he *does* and *undergoes*; he is the Kingdom he proclaims, the self-enacted parable of God which he speaks; he is himself as the crucified and resurrected Jesus. His titles may be substitutable and dispensable for identifying him. Messiah to some, he is Son of Man to others, Logos for others yet. But his passion and resurrection are not substitutable. He is the subject of his personal predicates and his doings and sufferings, and holds them together, essentially, rather than they him; he is the subject to whom descriptions are ascribed. Predicates are general, subjects particular. By contrast, in allegorical reading as it was revived in the eighteenth century, predicates or general characteristics have priority over particular subjects—the particulars are illustrations of a general "meaning." In literal reading, as in a realistic novel, the general is contained in the particular. It is that contrast which makes it so difficult to coordinate systematically and on even terms a literal-ascriptive-subject reading of the Gospels and a reading that has some other, general meaning for its semiotic referent—a goal that a number of liberal theolograms would like to accomplish. That of course makes for a difficult question: How may one so describe the predicates of Jesus that they are seen to be his, as it were owned by him, rather than, conversely, owning him? I shall return briefly to this point later on.

Third, once again, the consensus on which I have dwelled—not too illusorily, I hope—is a hermeneutical one and extends no further than that. As soon as we try to understand the text—as we are bound to do—under some such categorial scheme as "meaning" or "sense," and "truth" or "reference," and thus observe the logical distinction between these two categories, we find ourselves in a world of seemingly irreducible diversity. In other words, "literal" is not referentially univocal but embraces many possibilities. The Jesus whom we identify by his particular story is for some no more than this—the chief character in a narrative plot, the fiction of a savior figure as specific person, even if the whole beautiful story was generated, or more or less accidentally occasioned, by a charismatic figure who actually lived. Or the referent may be an actual historical figure, the historical person

Jesus who is isomorphic with (and not merely accidentally related to) some or all of the storied depictions. Or the status of this ascriptive subject may be that of a reality under an ontological or metaphysical scheme, such as one person in whom two natures are indissolubly and unabridgedly united. It may be other things also. In other words, *the consensus covers the literal reading or meaning of the New Testament stories about Jesus in an ascriptive mode, but not the reality status of the ascriptive subject Jesus* or even all the details of the *de*scriptive elements of the story.

To summarize: The continuity of Christian tradition in the West and now, I believe, beyond the West—lies in its textual or hermeneutical reading more than in the extratextual reference of the text, where we had often hoped to find it, or in the historical continuity of an experience that is supposedly continuous because it is the experience of him. The specificity and universality of Jesus Christ and the complex simplicity of his portrait are a matter, then, of the partial reiteration, rhetorical or didactic, of the text—sometimes in an aesthetic mode, always at the disciples' distance in a form of life, and to some extent in the fragmentary conceptual redescription that is the theologian's domain.

Have I trespassed? Have we given a name to "one unnamed or unknown," who even in the texts about him remains the subject who makes the texts in all their diversity and (finally, in the resurrection accounts) even in their confusion testimonies to himself—who identifies himself to us in them? The imperious ruler of Schweitzer's concluding remarks is the same as Karl Barth's judge who is judged in our place, the man who permits us, his poor brothers and sisters, to identify ourselves with him, though we are anything but identical with him, because he identifies himself with us: "While we were yet sinners Christ died for us." Perhaps then, by the grace of God, we are not trespassing when we urge the literal reading of the text in the ascriptive mode. We might then discover a variety of textual redescriptions, each partial, to be sure, and yet each a reiteration of the priority of the same ascriptive subject in the text—the same unitary, storied identity from a particular vantage point.

As one example—a particularly instructive one—of just such a redescription, let me cite a section from the writing of a revered teacher and colleague of mine, H. Richard Niebuhr's *Christ and Culture*. What is interesting for present purposes in the brief section entitled "To-

wards a Definition of Christ" is Niebuhr's determination to see the
unity in the variety of Christianity by referring all of it to the New
Testament portrait, not to a historical reconstruction of the portrait. It
is, if you will, a hermeneutical rather than a historical procedure. He
deals with the text as a finished product and inquires into its salient
formal, descriptive features. For that reason, Niebuhr asks not so much
what unitary features may be derived from this portrait for the Christian religion as a historical or phenomenological totality, but how the
unity and diversity of the religion may be related to the textual person
of Jesus, assuming that *it* may be discerned and discerned indeed as
one. "There always remain the original portraits with which all later
pictures may be compared and by which all caricatures may be cor-
rected. And in these original portraits he is recognizably one and the
same."[6] Niebuhr grants that every description is an interpretation but
is confident that it can be "an interpretation of the objective reality."

Next, Niebuhr indicates the perspective from which he tries to understand the unitary figure in his unitary story, while proposing that
such a limited perspective does not signify the collapse of Christian
continuity into culturally relativist isolation. His own approach to a
description (his pre-understanding?) is that of a moralist, one who
defines Christ by his virtues. He then takes two steps of considerable
interest. First, he appropriates various proposals about these virtues
or qualities of character made by liberal historians and their not-so-
liberal historical successors: Adolf von Harnack on Christ's virtue of
love, Albert Schweitzer on his virtue of extreme hope, and Rudolf
Bultmann on the virtue of radical obedience in him. This appropriation
is a simple device, for Niebuhr finds that there is something in each
of these descriptions—though not everything, as their authors imag-
ined. It is an especially striking device, however, because in this way
Niebuhr in effect combines two procedures which have frequently been
sharply opposed to each other. Historical-critical inquiry has every
right to be called a method. It has canons for what is evidence, for
analyzing the authenticity of sources. Hermeneutics, by contrast, has
no set of agreed-upon principles or procedures except that a text or a
discourse is to be understood in some extended context other than
merely its original historical setting and is to be seen therefore as a
linguistic world with an integrity of its own. But that is not a method.
But Niebuhr does *in fact*, though not by any announced procedure,
combine the textual portrait with the yield of a number of historical

analyses, thereby reattaching the result of the historian's analysis, his kind of literal reading, to the referent who may be indeed be the Jesus of history but may also be the Jesus Christ of tradition. While the generic features of this portrait in a moralist's redescription are clear, its referent may be much more mysterious, and his status indeterminate in comparison to the usually adduced modern options. Niebuhr takes each of these virtues—love, hope, obedience—and suggests that their radicality in each case lies not in the extremism of Jesus' commitment to each but in the directedness of each to God. Of each, one may say what is properly said in the case of his love: "There seems . . . to be no other adequate way to describe Jesus as having the virtue of love than to say that his love was that of the Son of God. It was not love but God that filled his soul. . . . Thus any one of the virtues of Jesus may be taken as the key to the understanding of his character and teaching; but each is intelligible in its apparent radicalism only as a relation to God."[7] "Yet this is only half the meaning of Christ considered morally. . . . Because he is the moral Son of God in his love, hope, faith, obedience, and humility in the presence of God, therefore he is the moral mediator of the Father's will toward men. Because he loves the Father with the perfection of human *eros*, therefore he loves men with the perfection of divine *agape*." Sonship to God involves him in "the double movement—with men toward God, with God toward men. . . . Jesus Christ is not a median figure, half God, half man; he is a single person wholly directed in his unity with the Father toward men. He is mediatorial, not median."[8]

Niebuhr, as a moral theologian, helps us move from *ascriptive* literalism to an appropriate form of *descriptive* literalism; and he helps us see that the textual, narrated unity of the person is so strong that divine and human are held together because they are predicates that are his as subject. It is exceedingly doubtful to my mind that any such unity can be reached by juxtaposing a "faith method" and "historical method," by trying to unite the Jesus of history with the Christ of faith. Two methods don't result in one person. Methods refer to modes or theories of explanation, not to answers to questions of identity.

Niebuhr said he looked at the text as a moralist, but that view would have to be supplemented by others. Well, why not? Just as historians and moralists may converge by uniting descriptive with ascriptive literalism in the redescription of a particular figure from the past, so may metaphysicians and moralists, dogmatic theologians and historians.

The proof of the pudding is in the eating, not in any printed recipe. The task of the redescription of Jesus will remain unfinished as long as history lasts, but that is *not at all* to claim that the conceptual bond of redescription woven by the very linguistic continuity of the community pledged to him cannot adopt for itself the culturally relative forms of that history. There is no contradiction in principle between the hermeneutical procedures of ascriptive literalism in Christology and the methods of other subdisciplines that produce specific cultural articulations that enter into the statement and restatement of Christology.

Appendix C ///////////// Eberhard Busch's
Biography of Karl Barth ///////////

When Friedrich Schleiermacher, the greatest systematic theologian of the nineteenth century, died, his reputation went into decline from which it did not fully recover for two generations.[1] He was overshadowed by the ghost of Hegel, his rival and antagonist at the University of Berlin. Those who followed in his own footsteps at the time were for the most part colorless epigones who reduced his complex and profound thought to a minor, compromising scholasticism. It wasn't the first or last time that this happened. The truism is right: A great man condemns the rest of us to the task of understanding his thought, a job that usually turns out to be thoroughly thankless, at least in the first decade or so after his death. Certainly Karl Barth has so far suffered the fate of his great predecessor. In this country he was identified with "neo-orthodoxy," and its demise as a result of the radical 60's meant that his own complex, massive reflections were submerged and left to an array of residual Barthians. There are signs that he is being read again, but interest in him among mainline Protestants and Catholics still seems at a rather low ebb.

The publication of Eberhard Busch's biography of Barth is therefore most welcome. It is not a critical biography but a story woven together from a pastiche of Barth's own autobiographical snippets, reports and letters—an autobiography at a second hand. Busch, who was Barth's last assistant puts all these beads on two strands designed to show them off to maximum advantage. One is Barth's own persuasion, old-fashioned and Calvinist one way, almost aesthetic in another, that

Eberhard Busch, *Karl Barth: His Life and Letters and Autobiographical Texts*, trans. John Bowden (Philadelphia: Fortress Press, 1976). This review was originally published in the *Virginia Seminary Journal* (July 1978): 42–46, and later reprinted in *Karl Barth in Re-View*, ed. H.-Martin Rumscheidt (Pittsburgh: Pickwick Press, 1981), 95–116. It is reprinted here with the kind permission of the Pickwick Press.

earthly life is a pilgrimage with a cumulative pattern built into it which is only partially evident at any given time. Busch does his (very good and tactfully muted) best to make Barth's own life illustrate the thesis. The other strand consists of brief maps of Barth's theology, each corresponding to a specific stage of his life, so that his theology too becomes a "pilgrim's progress". This is very well done but for reasons to be touched on later may be too concentrated and specialized for those who do not already have some acquaintance with Barth's writing.

I

This book is obviously only part of the raw material for an eventual critical biography of Barth. Though it might make one wistful, it is probably just as well that the appearance of such an *oeuvre* should be postponed. A colorful, larger-than-life personality like Barth might tempt a biographer prematurely into writing either a traditional "life," a kind of adulatory, Victorian character account, or into something like Lytton Strachey's elegant and skeptical transformation of the genre into iconoclastic motivational inquiry. Either performance would be a disservice, and certainly Barth's own brief forays into biographical description, for instance, in *Protestant Theology in the Nineteenth Century*, indulge neither in hero worship nor in motivational muckraking. One can only hope that his eventual biographer(s) will combine a healthy sense for the significance and power of Barth's accomplishment with some critical distancing tools which would also serve to provide illuminating context, for example, psychobiography or sociobiography. (But he/she had better also be aware of the limitations of these procedures!) But our day is probably too close for that, and this is indeed sad because Barth was an extraordinarily fascinating and complex person about whom one wants to know more. Had he not been a theologian, he would have been more widely recognized as one of the towering minds of the twentieth century. But it is precisely his overpowering quality that makes it necessary to gain some distance from him before one can have the confidence that one has put him in the right critical context. In the meantime Busch's book is a fascinating account, at once preliminary and yet also of abiding value.

Even the judgment of Barth's complexity has to be qualified. Certainly he was complicated and not always genial in his personal relations, in his curious mixture of candor and reserve, self-confidence and self-ironization, sharp polemical thrust and contrasting breadth of imagination and sympathy. But he was forcefully clear, even simple in other respects. His theological purpose was clearly singleminded, and through all his internal revolutions and revisions he exhibits a striking continuity, even though it would be difficult to state it in a way that is neither misleading nor uninformatively flat-footed. As a theological advocate or opponent, as an actor on the public stage, he never left anybody in doubt where he stood on any specific theological, political or economic issue of the day. He often drove toward a logic of extremes, and often the extremes would be simultaneous and mutually contrary. (For example, Franz Overbeck's atheism and J. C. Blumhardt's conservative eschatological prophecy appealed to him equally and for the same eschatological reasons in the 1920's.) But sooner or later he would discover his own position in the dialectical to-and-fro and defend it with the same tenacity that had gone into the labor of discovery. He was definitely not one ever to be pulled here and there "on the boundary," theologically, politically or in personal life. He was decisive, and could be frustratingly, even infuriatingly contrary and stubborn. Busch reports that on one occasion the church historian Hans von Campenhausen "quivered with anger because Karl Barth gave his political views in such a way that those who differed were necessarily put in question" (p. 405). This was over Barth's vehement opposition in 1954 against Adenauer's and the Eisenhower Administration's policy of rearming West Germany.

In short, what comes through in this autobiography-at-second-hand is an astonishingly strong, forceful personality, at once complex and yet extraordinarily singleminded in the work he considered important. Again and again, Busch spotlights Barth's complete dedication to his vocation, dogmatic theology, as his particular service within the Christian community, the Church. That was obviously his primary community, even if he was also passionately, if to some extent skeptically, engaged in political society, and to a lesser extent in the life of culture. When he wasn't working at his academic chores he was active in church life and in the world of affairs. He was constantly, though apparently not frenetically, engaged: One is not surprised to learn from the *Church Dogmatics* that Barth, unlike most other modern theologians, put sloth as high as pride on his list of sins. In this, as in many other ways, he was very much the Reformed Churchman, a species that has not often been accused of laziness. Reading Busch's book one gets a sense of deep-rooted and vigorous but thoroughly worldly and always activist rather than contemplative or spiritualistic piety at work. It seems to have been a piety that knew all about its own skepticism or "bad faith," but had put it in back of itself with complete confidence. This kind of temperament was bound to be utterly dismaying to much of the liberal religious sensibility with its critical tentativeness and its fears of professing more than one believes or practises and landing in hypocrisy as a result.

In a parallel fashion one has the impression that Barth was a man for whom overt force of character and the exercise of vocation, rather than internal self-consciousness, self-probing or the tensions of "self-transcendence" were the hallmarks of being human and of his own humanity. (One suspects that he would not have been a very patient subject in psychoanalysis.) Likewise, his relations with others, including many long and loyal friendships with other theologians and pastors, seem to have been forged through a sense of common vocation and common moral tasks, rather than through the art of mutual personal cultivation or direct in-depth "encounter." His intimate relation with his long-time assistant, Charlotte von Kirschbaum, was in its way perhaps the most striking instance of the first type of relationship in his life; his sad misrelation to his wife was his paradigmatic failure in the other kind. Future biographers will have to undertake some exceedingly painful inquiries about these matters. To what extent did a sense of shared vocation govern even his intimately personal, sexual life?

How much perspective Barth had on himself is a difficult question. He was aware of, and sometimes bothered by, the fact that his relations to people, even long-held friendships, could go sour; there is at least one wistful remark that "my life's work seems to lack a certain attraction; indeed, one characteristic of it seems to be a certain explosive or at any rate centrifugal effect" (p. 249; cf. p. 229). He seemed to sense that people felt threatened and overwhelmed by him, and at least later in life he tried to guard himself and others against his own forcefulness with an increasingly fatherly attitude. He also tried to ward off the temptations of fame, including the sycophancy of "Barthians." How successful these endeavors were is hard to estimate from Busch's account. Certainly, Barth actually relished opposition even though he could drive opponents to distraction by his confidence that he was right. Equally surely he was no fanatic, even if he was headstrong and willful, especially in his younger years. His protective device against his own, as well as others', pretensions was frequent ironization, self-ironization and self-needling, sometimes in mock-solemn, mock-elevated language. It is an interesting but double-edged instrument, and it says much about Barth. People often try to exorcise their all too real demons by mocking them either in deliberate exaggeration or in transparently tongue-in-cheek denial. Barth did both. To a friend reproaching him for always wanting to be right "he retorted with a chuckle: 'But I always *am* right' " (p. 395). His notoriously vehement polemical pamphlet of 1934 against Emil Brunner (*No! Reply to Emil Brunner*), written at a time when he was fiercely and combatively tilting with a whole host of opponents, he introduced with the words: "I am by nature a gentle being and completely disinclined toward all unnecessary quarrels." One is reminded of a painfully jocose and all too revelatory remark by former Israeli Foreign Minister Moshe Dayan to then Secretary of State Cyrus Vance: "Mr. Secretary, as soon as you accept our position we shall be in perfect accord." Vance was not amused. Nor were all of Barth's contemporaries. Ritual exorcism by humor all too often reaffirms the tenant rights of the very demons seemingly expelled, especially in the case of forceful personalities.

II

But when all is said and done, Barth's astonishing confidence and ego strength served him well in many ways. They were in large part a function of a sense of identity so secure that he could throughout all his life castigate the narrower, ungenerous parts of the very heritage that helped supply it in the first place. He was a loyal, but very critically loyal, Swiss Reformed Churchman all his life, and as such he became a dedicated citizen of the universal church of Jesus Christ within a world he saw as one in its suffering and promise. More than anything else the Busch biography is the personal detailing of that life vocation from Barth's perspective, with all the power of his vigorous personality manifest.

Most readers will find the sections detailing his passionate break with theological liberalism and his equally passionate fight against the inhumanity of the Nazi regime the most engrossing. To summarize briefly what was at stake in those battles is impossible. Especially in regard to his epoch-making break with theological liberalism, between

1915 and 1922, too many factors enter the picture. For example, there is the part played by Barth's vigorous (and life-long) socialist and anti-imperialist political convictions, fairly unusual for a Protestant minister in Switzerland and certainly much more so in Germany at the time. At some stages he did, at others he did not relate them to his theological revolt. Both in those and later years Barth revised again and again the rationale of his drastic theological turn. Furthermore he was at that time writing very much as a theological pastor to other pastors, passionately and explosively, so that a thumbnail sketch of his prose is inappropriate to the point of being misleading.

But one theme, as important as any Barth pursued throughout that period, was that knowledge of and relationship with God are not a given, natural state of affairs to be confidently enjoyed and nourished, but a complete crisis in our being. For this relation is at once inescapable and deeply problematical because it is embodied not in our strengths and achievements but in the ultimate and ineluctable limits of our lives and capacities. In his own very Christian and very individual way, he was stating the general ideological crisis of many Europeans in the wake of the First World War, which Expressionists and radical socialists had already presaged in earlier days. Certainly in the famous second edition of his *The Epistle to the Romans*, Barth's deliberately abrupt and staccato style, his distended, exaggerated metaphors and the provocative, allusive force of his rhetoric are all strikingly reminiscent of Expressionism, although he soon abandoned that mode and (once more astonishingly similar to an identical turn in contemporary German letters), moved on to the style of a *neue Sachlichkeit*. In any event, his statement of the crisis was indeed thoroughly Christian: The crisis of faith, it was important to him to say is not the effect of our *not* knowing God but, on the contrary, of the fact that even in our skepticism we cannot get rid of him. "Don't things get dangerous only *if* and *because* God is?" (p. 91). Implied is not only that God is inescapable but that the condition for knowing God, and even knowing that we do *not* know him, is God himself. In this view even the radical skepticism of "modernity," much as it is to be preferred to liberal or conservative religious self-confidence or complacency about divine-human contact, is child's play compared to the absolute crisis under God, the discovery at the limit of our lives that the absolutely transcendent is inescapable, and that it is its ingression upon us through our questioning, and not our own questioning itself, that makes our whole being a critical problem.

Barth had a hard time expressing this conviction in a way that suited him theologically, for it contained a basic ambiguity that cried out not only for clarification but, even more, decision. He could move in one of two and only two directions. He could quite self-consciously be a Christian theologian within the framework of the ideological and cultural crisis of "modern Western man." In that case his theology would have become an ambitious endeavor to interpret cultural and ecclesiastical outlooks and communities to each other, trying to show that Christianity is the ultimate cutting edge of the radical, *autonomous* quest for meaning and self-understanding of modern despisers and, for that matter, non-despisers of religion. Not as Christians but simply as finite, yet autonomous human beings we are finally constituted as an insoluble question to ourselves; and the question that we ourselves are is at the same time our question about God which we cannot answer. Of our own momentum we are driven to the desperate edge of the absolutely transcendent. The interpretation of Christianity would in that case be constituted by an anthropo-theology, in which understanding of God and genuinely authentic human self-understanding would be mutually indispensable, each being interpreted through the other. Our autonomous, self- and God-questioning would at the same time be understood at its radical edge as our being questioned by God.

On the other hand, he could decide that the relation between the self-description of Christianity and all *autonomously* conceived human, cultural quests for ultimate meaning is indirect, that they are logically diverse even when they are existentially connected, that is to say, even when they reside within the same breast. In that case one could not systematically correlate the two. This in turn has two consequences. First, a Christian theologian opting for this alternative would presumably give priority to Christian self-description, so that description of the general human condition, whether in "crisis" or not, would be dependent on that prior description. From that vantage point, and given that a Christian outlook is universal in scope, he would therefore not view the quest for self-understanding or ultimate meaning as an autonomous enterprise at all. Rather, he would refer it strictly to the distinctive judgment and saving grace of God in Jesus Christ as the sole and encompassing context within which to reflect on all such matters. But, secondly, he would then in effect agree with the increasing number of post-Christian "secularists" that the time was past (if indeed it had ever existed) when Christianity could supply either the symbolic form or the substantive answer to an *autonomously* conceived cultural, anthropological quest for ultimate meaning and self-understanding.

The whole conceptual scheme or framework of a self-involving "question and answer" pattern or of the "hermeneutical circle" between an existential pre-understanding and the understanding of the Christian message would then lose its supposed status as *the* indispensable conceptual or dialectical instrument for thinking Christianly. ... In some conditions such talk might be appropriate, in others not. Rather, Christian theology must in the first place pay heed to the language of the Christian community from the Bible to modernity, understood as an organic pattern possessing its own integrity, its own complex logic and highly varying relation to other forms of language and life.

These were the options that Barth's early, anti-liberal protest opened up to him. His *Romans* commentary and other contemporary writings left the issue unresolved under the apparent solution that the gospel constitutes the "absolute crisis" of autonomous secular as well as religious humanity. This rather broad notion and others like it merely served to veil, to a surprising degree, the fact that the choice between the two positions just outlined really cut to the bone. This intellectual confusion was no doubt in part a function of the existentially tough character of the decision that was involved. Increasingly, painstakingly, and then more and more decisively Barth opted for the second alternative. Eventually, in the early 1930's, as his dogmatic theology developed and under the impact not only of theological but political controversy against the intrusion of Nazi ideology into the church, he came to put it in that extraordinary, one-sided, controversial dogmatic-theological fashion that was to become his hallmark: Jesus Christ, he said, as witnessed in all of Scripture, is the one and only Word of God and the only source for the knowledge of God. Here God is present and known to us, and the only logical presupposition for this presence and this knowledge is—itself. For this unique thing there can be no set preconditions; it creates its own. No natural theology, no anthropology, no characterization of the human condition, no ideology or world view can set the conditions for theology or knowledge of God.

Autonomous anthropology and Christian theology cannot be understood as mutually implicated, nor is there any one specific conceptual framework that must be *the* precondition for making theological discourse meaningful.

Not only was this thesis vehemently controverted at the time; all of its forms: that of totally Christ-focused knowledge of God; the logical (though not existential) discontinuity between such Christocentric theology and an independent anthropology or cultural world view; the dominance of the constancy of Christological affirmation over the variableness of its conceptual expressions and anthropological correlations; and Barth's earlier, apparent taking-for-granted that God is, despite or even in our not knowing him, are largely responsible for the wide rejection of Barth's thought since his death. But at the time he set them forth they were expressions of an enormous theological vitality which became a powerful force on behalf of an embattled cause.

Theologically and also politically his thesis served as a rallying point for those who wished to resist firmly the attribution of even secondary divine "revelatory" status to the nationalistic fanaticism that took possession of Germany in 1933 under Hitler. They were a small group, and they needed all the courage they could muster. The great danger to the Church's witness, as Barth saw clearly, was not the stupid and fanatical "German Christian movement" which envisioned Nazism as the fulfillment of Christianity (yes, there actually were those!) but the compromisers who saw two sources for discerning the will and action of God—the Bible, but also the historical events of time, nation and culture. Quite naturally then–he reserved his most vehement polemics for those whom he thought most consistent in compromising the exclusive sovereignty of the divine Word in their dogmatic as well as their political theology. In dogmatics they asserted the indispensable methodological coherence of autonomous anthropology, the fruit of reflexive analysis of subjectivity and of contemporary culture, with a biblical doctrine of God's relation to man. They then quite logically united this dogmatic compromise to a similar political-theological one for which (again) God made himself known in Scripture but also in the special vocation, culture and laws of particular nations at particular times. Concretely, of course, the latter claim meant in 1933 that the German "national renewal" was being acclaimed as divinely sanctioned. The man who represented this compromising combination most consistently and disastrously in Barth's view in the early and mid 1930's was his former ally in the earlier days of the "dialectical theology," Friedrich Gogarten. In the face of this sort of thing Barth passionately asserted and reasserted the exclusive sovereignty of the one Word of God, exclusively testified to in Scripture. He asserted and reasserted the indirect identity of the whole Bible, both Old and New Testaments, with the one and only Word of God incarnate in Jesus of Nazareth.

In those days, a small embattled minority took heart not only from the singleminded tenacity and clarity of Barth's thesis but from his boldness (some called it brashness). In 1932, in the preface to the first volume of his *Church Dogmatics*, he said that anyone waiting for the Protestant church to take itself (i.e., its dogmatic-theological task) seriously would have to wait until doomsday, "unless in all modesty he dares in his own place and as well as he knows how, to *be* that church." For a minority voice to assume that it actually represents—not to say embodies—the group in which a majority diverges from him is a bold claim. Barth extended it quite naturally from the dogmatic-theological to the political-theological arena. For him it was all of one piece, given the force of his governing conviction about the sole sovereignty of the Word of God and its compelling character.

The trouble was that others never quite saw matters in the same almost ruthlessly single-minded way; nor could they use in the same fashion the strange-appearing and consistent dogmatic language which Barth now came to employ. Even people who agreed with him in the German church struggle dissented from his theological rationale for his stand. And as time went on and the echoes of that battle (with its arguments over the mystification and demystification of national culture) faded, more and more people rejected Barth's theological insistence that just as there can be no "natural theology" for Christians, so there can be no systematic "pre-understanding," no single, specific, consistently used conceptual scheme, no independent or semi-independent anthropology, hermeneutics, ontology or whatever, in terms of which Christian language and Christian claims must be cast in order to be meaningful. Despite his eminence and the sheer weight of his presence on the theological scene, he always remained a curiously isolated figure. Even if he set the terms of the argument, and to a large extent he did, most people took the other side, to which Rudolf Bultmann eventually gave representative expression with his call for an existential pre-understanding and a consistent conceptual structure, that of Existentialist philosophy, in terms of which to interpret the New Testament message in modern day.

Busch's detailed account, or rather his shaping of Barth's own fragmentary accounts of the theoretical and practical struggles from the break with liberalism to the end of the Second World War, a period of about thirty years, is admirably done and conveys the spirit and passion of that epoch in theology, politics and Barth's personal life. It makes compelling reading in the midst of some things that do not. Busch is an almost painfully conscientious and fair-minded author. Not a single individual who crossed Barth's path and no event, no matter how minute, seems to be left out. The index of persons alone comes to almost twelve double column, small print pages in the German original. For the American reader these details of the Swiss and German landscape, theological, ecclesiastical, and academic, are apt to prove burdensome. But this is a minor problem. Perseverance will not really be difficult and will pay off.

III

There is however another and very large problem about the book. It was virtually inescapable, so that Busch cannot be faulted for it. Readers of Barth's *Church Dogmatics* usually come up with the same experience: Whether one agrees with Barth or not, and despite the endless repetition of themes and the stylistic heaviness, much increased by the translation, which loses the almost colloquial vigor of the German original, there is an increasingly compelling, engrossing quality to the material. And it is much more accessible than much modern theology: Even the technical terms don't lose sight of ordinary language, and Barth possesses astonishing descriptive powers. But then, as one tries to restate it afterwards the material dies on one's hands. It can be done, but there is nothing as wooden to read as one's own or others' restatements of Barth's terms, his technical themes and their development. It is as though he had preempted that particular language and its deployment. For that reason reading "Barthians," unlike Barth himself, can often be painfully boring.

On the other hand, brief summary reports of what he wrote are apt to be uninformative to the point of being virtually hermetic, except for those who are already "in" on it. Busch renders a real service by reporting the development of Barth's theology at every stage of his life. He is a real expert and obviously knows the massive material inside out. But his summary reports are almost always of the hermetic variety, and there is nothing he could have done about it. Barth's theology had some persistent, simple themes. But their development was extremely complex and subtle, and therein lies its power, richness, originality and imaginativeness. (Even Barth's own occasional brief summaries of his thought tend to lack the force and persuasiveness of the *Dogmatics*.)

Why the prolixity of the *Church Dogmatics*? Why its peculiar character of being at once accessible and yet so difficult to do justice to in exposition and commentary? Barth was naturally talkative, and the *Dogmatics* was developed out of his class lectures. Moreover, he obviously felt an unusual fascination, even for a theologian, with the sheer beauty, the sublime fitness and also the rational availability of the *loci* of Christian dogma. This almost aesthetic passion extended most especially to the classical themes of Christian doctrine that tend to get short shrift in modern theology, e.g., the Trinity, Predestination. In addition, it has to be remembered that Barth was not a systematic but a dogmatic theologian, so that the whole substance of Christian theology could for him be mirrored in a distinct way in every one of its major, quasi-independent topics. (And that obviously makes for length!) This is especially true of the doctrines of predestinating grace (vol. II, 2) and reconciliation (IV, 1–IV, 4), but it was already true of the prolegomena to the whole work, vols. I,1 and I,2. Despite their vast difference over the possibility of system-building, there are shades here of Hegel, Barth's favorite philosopher, who also saw everything that is knowable implied and potentially contained in any single instance of it, and who also wrote or spoke at inordinate length, as though intoxicated by his vision.

But when all is said and done, there is a more important consideration. Barth was about the business of conceptual description: He took the classical themes of communal Christian language molded by the Bible, tradition and constant usage in worship, practice, instruction and controversy, and he restated or redescribed them, rather than evolving arguments on their behalf. It was of the utmost importance to him that this communal language, especially its biblical *fons et origo*, which, as we have noted, he saw as indirectly one with the Word of God, had an integrity of its own: It was irreducible. But in that case its lengthy, even leisurely unfolding was equally indispensable. For he was restating or re-using a language that had once been accustomed talk, both in first-order use in ordinary or real life, and in second-order technical theological reflection, but had now for a long time, perhaps more than 250 years, been receding from natural familiarity, certainly in theological discourse. So Barth had as it were to recreate a universe of discourse, and he had to put the reader in the middle of that world, instructing him in the use of that language by showing him how— extensively, and not only by stating the rules or principles of the discourse. In that respect he was almost totally different from the much less fluid and much more exclusively second-order as well as single-conceptual-system procedure of virtually all of his modern colleagues. This is *not* to say that he was basically less consistent than they. The design that governed Barth's manifold and changing procedures re-mained very much the same from the first volume of *Church Dogmatics* in 1932 onwards. But unlike others, it was of the essence of his design that it could not be stated apart from its specific unfolding or descrip-tion without losing its force.

At first Barth had employed a linguistic or cognitive model of a very specific kind in the methodological, introductory part of his dogmatic project, where he raised the question of the internal logic governing the use of dogmatic language. The presence of God's Word to hu-mankind, directly in Jesus Christ and indirectly in Scripture and in the church's contemporary preaching, was, he suggested, to be con-ceived after the fashion of the free self-presentation or self-reiteration of a subject in performative utterance, so that no ultimate self-differentiation could be made between God's self-expressive language, his activity, and himself. God's Word is God himself in the form of his own spiritual speech-act. Faith in or knowledge of that divine presence was likewise a form of spiritual activity or understanding, one that united intellectual comprehension and existential acknowl-edgment of that present Word with personal trust and obedience to it.

There was no break, no sharp rupture, or later retraction between the methodological introduction and the subsequent content of the *Church Dogmatics*. However, Barth's vision and statement of the world of discourse of which he was rendering an account became increasingly and self-consciously temporal rather than cognitivist. It was a world in which time elapsed, and that was of its very essence, so that he had both to proceed diachronically in describing it and take temporality into account in articulating the most appropriate and least distorting methods. He no longer saw the whole range of divine-human commerce, as it is described in the language of the church, simply under the auspices of an "act" of divine self-projection together with its fit apprehension ("revelation"). Rather, both methodologically and substantively that world of discourse could only be described piecemeal fashion, an important reason for his not developing a system and (again) for his prolixity. Its primary first-order depiction was narrative, the narrative originally told in the Old and New Testaments (though unlike Barthians and neo-orthodox theologians he never systematized the Bible into a single "biblical point of view" or a *"Heilsgeschichte"*). This persuasion of a temporal world became increasingly evident in volumes II, 2; III, 1, and IV. Increasingly he incorporated the retelling of biblical narratives, sometimes in the main text (as in IV), sometimes (as in II, 2 and III, 1) in those enormous small print *excursus* in which he handles his exegesis of the Bible, as well as his discussions with past and present conversation partners.

It was as though even the concepts he employed flowed, and we are watching them move in their own medium, as figurations of motion in time. For this purpose Barth employed a variety of devices, of which I can merely mention two. "Analogy" is an analytical, technical category which he employed increasingly, beginning with his book on Anselm of Canterbury, *Fides Quaerens Intellectum* and the first volume of the *Church Dogmatics*, to help state the mutual fitness, through God's grace, of God and humanity, in other words, their sharing a common narrative. This contrasted with his earlier (1920's) anti-liberal use of the category and procedure called "dialectic," which served as a name for those thought sequences that indicate at once an absolute distance and a completely static as well as largely negative coinherence of God and humanity. Later in Barth's development, "dialectic" instead became an important subordinate device (and formal category) in the service of "analogy," redescribing conceptually and by means of a series of fluid juxtapositions (of figures, images, events, persons, points of view) the teleological, temporal flow of the divine-human relation, of which the New Testament depiction of Jesus Christ gives at once the foundation and the aim. Analogy and dialectic, like all other technical devices, become expressions of his persuasion that that relation is properly and in the first place narrated, that it can indeed be redescribed, but only secondarily and fragmentarily, even though appropriately, and that it cannot in the first place be argued. Barth's theology proceeds by narrative and conceptually descriptive statement rather than by argument or by way of an explanatory theory under-girding the description's real or logical possibility. (Not even the doc-trine of predestinating grace [vol. II, 2] serves an all-embracing explanatory function, although Barth sometimes and inconsistently came close to saying so.)

In the process of this fragmentary, piecemeal description or rede-scription of the temporal world of eternal grace, Barth employs his battery of auxiliary instruments to indicate two things simultaneously: (1) that this world is a world with its own linguistic integrity, much as a literary art work is a consistent world in its own right, one that we can have only under a depiction, under its own particular depiction and not any other, and certainly not in pre-linguistic immediacy or in experience without depiction; but (2) that unlike any other depicted world it is the one common world in which we all live and move and have our being. To indicate all this he will use scriptural exegesis to illustrate his themes; he will do ethics to indicate that this narrated, narratable world is at the same time the ordinary world in which we are responsible for our actions; and he will do *ad hoc* apologetics, in order to throw into relief particular features of this world by distancing them from or approximating them to other descriptions of the same or other linguistic worlds. In such cases, and in very few others, he engages in argument, usually of a highly dialectical kind, and usually to indicate distance and proximity at the same time. But none of these other descriptions or, for that matter, argument with them can serve as a "pre-description" for the world of Christian discourse which is also this common world, for to claim that it can would mean stepping outside that encompassing world; and that by definition is impossible.

All of this of course is done in the conviction that this world of discourse is indeed descriptively accessible. Ever since his book on Anselm's *Proslogion's* argument for the existence of God, Barth re-garded reason as conceptually descriptive effort, as one, though only one, of the legitimate shapes of faith, the shape taken by the theological endeavor. But the appropriate ruled language use of that description is irreducible to any other. Hence he thought that while any and all technical philosophical concepts and conceptual schemes could be em-ployed in Christian theology, they could only be used formally: One must remain agnostic about all their material claims to be describing the "real" world, even or especially when these schemes are anthropological and metaphysical in nature; and Barth did among other ones use anthropological and metaphysical schemes in his theology. In order not to become trapped by his philosophy, it is best for a theologian to be philosophically eclectic, in any given case employing the particular "conceptuality" or conceptualities (to put it in the German mode) that serve best to cast into relief the particular theological subject matter under consideration. The subject matter governs concepts as well as method, not vice versa.

Professor Maurice Wiles once suggested (*The Remaking of Christian Doctrine*, 1974, pp. 24f) that Barth is best read as a poet among theologians, much as Arnold Toynbee should be read as a poet among historians rather than as a historian. Barth himself spoke relatively infrequently, though most appreciatively, of the use of imagination in theology. But he knew how to use it, which is more to the point. One is tempted to speak of his work as the product of "dogmatic imagination," if possible pejorative overtones of that awkward construction may be disallowed in advance. In much the same way as the now old-fashioned "newer" literary critics he set forth a textual world which he refused to understand by paraphrase, or by transposition or "translation" into some other context but interpreted in second-order reflection with the aid of an array of formal, technical tools. Sometimes the second-order talk merged with imaginative restatements, in various modes, of parts of the original narrative to which it is fitly related. In a sense, then, he was indeed a poet, setting forth mimetically a world of discourse, but with a clear and strong sense of the appropriate coinherence of technical theological analysis with its more imaginative counterpart. The two are carefully crafted together, and together they are governed by the controlling subject matter.

There are many different ways of doing theology, many controlling concerns and outlooks, and one may not want to agree with Barth's governing vision, or with his particular exercise of imagination or of rationality or both together. But can really strong theology be any less? Can it be less than *some* form of this combination?

/ / / /

The prolixity and accessibility of Barth's theology, as well as the difficulty of secondhand restatement, are all then in the nature of the case. They are functions of the distinctive, even classic character of

Barth's work. But they forced an impossible task on Eberhard Busch when he tried to summarize the stages of Barth's theologizing. The enduring excellence of this book is therefore neither that it gives us a critical perspective on Barth the man, nor that it succeeds at a less than highly technical level of joining the theology to the man. But in between there can be a statement of Barth's life as his own Christian vocational task, as his pilgrimage. At that significant level Busch could not have done better. His care and craftsmanship and the breadth of his work in the sources are such that his work is not likely to be superseded in this respect, even by a critical biography.

Notes ////////////

CHAPTER 1. PROPOSAL FOR A PROJECT

1 Hans W. Frei, *The Identity of Jesus Christ* (Philadelphia: Fortress Press, 1975).
2 Hans W. Frei, *The Eclipse of Biblical Narrative* (New Haven: Yale University Press, 1975).
3 Hans W. Frei, "David Friedrich Strauss," in *Nineteenth-Century Religious Thought in the West*, ed. N. Smart et al., vol. 1 (Cambridge: Cambridge University Press, 1985), pp. 215–60.
4 Hans W. Frei, "The 'Literal Reading' of Biblical Narrative in the Christian Tradition: Does It Stretch or Will It Break?" in *The Bible and the Narrative Tradition*, ed. Frank McConnell (Oxford: Oxford University Press, 1985), pp. 36–77.

CHAPTER 2. INTRODUCTION

1 David Friedrich Strauss, *The Christ of Faith and the Jesus of History*, trans. Leander E. Keck (Philadelphia: Fortress Press, 1977), p. 5.
2 Karl Barth, *Protestant Theology in the Nineteenth Century*, trans. Brian Cozens (London: SCM Press, 1972), p. 568.
3 Clifford Geertz, *The Interpretation of Cultures* (New York: Basic Books, 1973), pp. 3–30.
4 Ibid., pp. 12–13.
5 Ibid., p. 14.
6 Brevard Childs, "The Sensus Literalis of Scripture: An Ancient and Modern Problem," in *Beiträge zur Alttestamentlichen Theologie: Festschrift für Walther Zimmerli zum 70 Geburstag*, ed. Herbert Donner (Göttingen: Vandanhoeck & Ruprecht, 1976), pp. 80–93.
7 Charles M. Wood, *The Formation of Christian Understanding* (Philadelphia: Westminster Press, 1981).
8 Frank Kermode, *The Genesis of Secrecy* (Cambridge: Harvard University Press, 1979).

CHAPTER 3. THEOLOGY, PHILOSOPHY, AND CHRISTIAN SELF-DESCRIPTION

1 Carl Henry, *God, Revelation and Authority* (Waco: Word Books, 1976), vol. 1, p. 200.
2 Ibid., pp. 206–7.
3 David Tracy, *Blessed Rage for Order* (New York: Seabury Press, 1975), pp. 55ff.
4 Clifford Geertz, "Religion as a Cultural System," *The Interpretation of Cultures* (New York: Basic Books, 1973), pp. 89ff.

CHAPTER 4. FIVE TYPES OF THEOLOGY

1 Gordon Kaufmann, *An Essay on Theological Method* (Chico, Calif.: Scholars Press, 1975), p. 67.
2 David Tracy, *Blessed Rage for Order* (New York: Seabury Press, 1975), p. 34.
3 Ibid., pp. 70–71.
4 Paul Ricoeur, *Interpretation Theory* (Fort Worth: Texas Christian University Press, 1976).
5 Tracy, *Blessed Rage for Order*, p. 136.
6 Friedrich Schleiermacher, *The Christian Faith*, trans. H. R. Mackintosh and J. S. Stewart (Edinburgh: T. & T. Clark, 1928), p. 52.
7 Friedrich Schleiermacher, *On the Glaubenslehre: Two Letters to Dr. Lücke*, trans. James Duke and Francis S. Fiorenza (Chico, Calif.: Scholars Press, 1981). See, for instance, p. 81.
8 Schleiermacher, *The Christian Faith*, p. 29.
9 Karl Barth, *Church Dogmatics*, vol. 1, part 1, trans. G. T. Thomson (Edinburgh: T. & T. Clark, 1936), p. 1.
10 Ibid., pp. 7–9.
11 D. Z. Phillips, *Faith and Philosophical Enquiry* (New York: Schocken Books, 1979), p. 17.
12 Ibid., p. 15.
13 Ibid., p. 2.
14 See ibid., p. 3.
15 Ibid., pp. 4–5.
16 Peter Winch, *The Idea of a Social Science* (London: Routledge and Kegan Paul, 1958), pp. 100–101.
17 Phillips, *Faith and Philosophical Enquiry*, p. 9.
18 Ibid.
19 Ibid., p. 4.
20 Ibid., pp. 86–87.
21 Ibid., p. 87; emphasis added.
22 Ibid., pp. 96ff.

23 Ibid., p. 101.

24 Ibid., pp. 88f.

25 Ibid., p. 105.

CHAPTER 5. SOME IMPLICATIONS FOR BIBLICAL INTERPRETATION

1 David H. Kelsey, *The Uses of Scripture in Recent Theology* (Philadelphia: Fortress Press, 1975), chap. 5.

2 Harold Bloom, *A Map of Misreading* (New York: Oxford University Press, 1975).

3 Frank Kermode, *The Genesis of Secrecy* (Cambridge: Harvard University Press, 1979).

4 Harold Bloom, *The Anxiety of Influence* (New York: Oxford University Press, 1973).

5 David Tracy, *Blessed Rage for Order* (New York: Seabury Press, 1975), p. 128. The page references that follow in the text are also to this work.

6 Friedrich Schleiermacher, *The Christian Faith*, trans. H. R. Mackintosh and J. S. Stewart (Edinburgh: T. & T. Clark, 1928), p. 593.

CHAPTER 6. AD HOC CORRELATION

1 Friedrich Schleiermacher, *The Christian Faith*, trans. H. R. Mackintosh and J. S. Stewart (Edinburgh: T. & T. Clark, 1928), p. 125.

2 Ibid., p. 12.

3 Ibid., p. 13.

4 David Friedrich Strauss, *The Christ of Faith and the Jesus of History*, trans. Leander E. Keck (Philadelphia: Fortress Press, 1977), pp. 4–5.

5 Schleiermacher, *The Christian Faith*, p. 123.

6 Ibid., p. 361.

7 Ibid., p. 385.

8 Strauss, *The Christ of Faith and the Jesus of History*, pp. 35–36.

9 Karl Barth, *Church Dogmatics*, vol. 1, part 1, trans. G. T. Thomson (Edinburgh: T. & T. Clark, 1936), p. 1.

10 Ibid., p. 7.

11 Ibid., p. 8.

12 Karl Barth, *Church Dogmatics*, vol. 1, part 2, trans. G. W. Bromiley and T. F. Torrance (Edinburgh: T & T Clark, 1956), pp. 727, 729.

13 Ibid., pp. 730ff.

14 Ibid., p. 730. [Frei's manuscript contains a blank space at this point; he often carried a book with him to a lecture and read passages like this direct from the text. Barth lists a series of five informal rules; this passage summarizes the first of them.]

15 Bruce Marshall, *Christology in Conflict* (Oxford: Basil Blackwell, 1987), pp. 21–22.

16 David H. Kelsey, *The Uses of Scripture in Recent Theology* (Philadelphia: Fortress Press, 1975), p. 43.

CHAPTER 7. THE END OF ACADEMIC THEOLOGY?

1 Charles M. Wood. *The Formation of Christian Understanding* (Philadelphia: Westminster Press, 1981), p. 25.

2 Fergus Kerr, *Theology after Wittgenstein* (Oxford: Basil Blackwell, 1986), p. 181.

APPENDIX A. THEOLOGY IN THE UNIVERSITY

1 Claude Welch, *Protestant Thought in the Nineteenth Century*, 2 vols. (New Haven: Yale University Press, 1972, 1985).

2 Emanuel Hirsch, *Geschichte der neuern evangelischen Theologie*, 5 vols. (Gutersloh: C. Bertelsmann Verlag, 1949–54).

3 Cf. Friedrich Paulsen, *The German Universities and University Study*, trans. Frank Thilly (New York: Charles Scribner's Sons, 1906), p. 54: "The confessional character of the old territorial university was completely repudiated."

4 Anthony T. Kronman, *Max Weber* (Stanford: Stanford University Press, 1983), pp. 176ff.; Max Weber, *Economy and Society*, trans. Ephraim Fischoff (New York: Bedminster Press, 1968), pp. 1393ff.

5 See Ernst Rudolf Huber, *Deutsche Verfassungsgeschichte seit 1789*, vol. 1 (Stuttgart, 1957), pp. 265–69.

6 See the account of governmental interference in the university in the Restoration period after the Napoleonic Wars in Max Lenz, *Geschichte der königlichen Friedrich-Wilhelms-Universität zu Berlin* (Halle: Buchhandlung des Waisenhauses, 1910), vol. 2, part 1, chap. 2.

7 Fritz K. Ringer, *The Decline of the German Mandarins* (Cambridge: Harvard University Press, 1969).

8 Daniel Fallon, *The German University: An Heroic Ideal in Conflict with the Modern World* (Boulder: Colorado Associated University Press, 1980), p. 29.

9 E. L. Solte, *Theologie an der Universität. Staats und kirchenrechtliche Probleme der theologischen Fakultäten* (München: Claudius, 1971), p. 3.

10 Huber, p. 265.

11 Huber, pp. 450–74, esp. p. 463. For a brief account, see Robert Bigler, *The Politics of German Protestantism* (Berkeley: University of California Press, 1972), p. 39.

12 Helge Siemers and Hans-Richard Reuter, eds., *Theologie als Wissenschaft in der Gesellschaft* (Göttingen: Vandenhoeck and Ruprecht, 1970), p. 158.

13 Karl Barth, *Church Dogmatics*, vol. 1, part 1, trans. G. T. Thomson (Edinburgh: T. & T. Clark, 1936), p. 7.

14 E. L. Solte, *Theologie an der Universität*, pp. 10ff.

15 Johann Gottlieb Fichte, "Dedusierter Plan einer in Berline zuerrichtenden hoheren Lehranstalt" (1807), in *Die Idee der deutschen Universität: die fünf Grundschriften aus der Zeit ihrer Neu-Begründung durch Rlassischen Idealismus und romantischen Realismus*, ed. Ernst Anrich (Darmstadt: H. Gentner, 1956), pp. 127–217.

16 Ibid., pp. 154ff.

17 Friedrich Schleiermacher, *Brief Outline on the Study of Theology*, trans. Terrence N. Tice (Richmond: John Knox Press, 1966).

18 Friedrich Schleiermacher, *Gelegentliche Gedanken über Universitäten in deutschem Sinn. Nebst einem Anhang über eine neu zu errichtende* (Berlin: Realschulbuchhandlung, 1808).

19 Anrich, p. 238.

20 Ibid., pp. 257f.

21 Ibid., p. 528.

22 Schleiermacher, *Brief Outline*, paragraphs 1 and 5, pp. 19–20. [Frei has translated from the German edition.]

23 The famous exchange of letters between Harnack and Barth is included in James M. Robinson, *The Beginnings of Dialectical Theology* (Richmond: John Knox Press, 1968), pp. 165–87.

24 Austin M. Farrer, *The Glass of Vision* (London: Dacre Press, 1948).

25 See Wolfhart Pannenberg, *Theology and the Philosophy of Science*, trans. Francis McDonald (Philadelphia: Westminster Press, 1976); Basil Mitchell, *The Justification of Religious Belief* (New York: Oxford University Press, 1973). For an analysis of kinds of justification of religious belief and a comparison of explanation of religious belief with explanation in the philosophy of science and social science, I am indebted to the dissertation of Philip Clayton (now published as *Explanation from Physics to Theology: An Essay in Rationality and Religion* [New Haven: Yale University Press, 1989]).

26 Susan J. Hekman, *Weber, the Ideal Type and Contemporary Social Theory* (Notre Dame: University of Notre Dame Press, 1983), p. 147.

27 Clayton, *Explanation from Physics*, pp. 32, 60f.

APPENDIX B. THE ENCOUNTER OF JESUS WITH THE GERMAN ACADEMY

1 Albert Schweitzer, *The Quest for the Historical Jesus*, trans. W. Montgomery (New York: Macmillan, 1961), p. 403.

2 David Kelsey, *The Uses of Scripture in Recent Theology* (Philadelphia: Fortress Press, 1975), p. 48.

3 Wayne Meeks, *The Moral World of the First Christians* (Philadelphia: Westminster Press, 1986), p. 136.

4 Beryl Smalley, *The Study of the Bible in the Middle Ages*, 3d ed. (rev.) (Oxford: Basil Blackwell, 1984), pp. 83–111.

5 Stephen W. Sykes, *The Identity of Christianity* (London: S.P.C.K., 1984).

6 H. Richard Niebuhr, *Christ and Culture* (New York: Harper and Row, 1975), p. 13.

7 Ibid., pp. 19, 27.

8 Ibid., pp. 28–29.

Index ///////////